Shipwreck with Spectator

Shipwreck with Spectator

Paradigm of a Metaphor for Existence

Hans Blumenberg

translated by Steven Rendall

The MIT Press
Cambridge, Massachusetts
London, England

This book was set in Bembo by The MIT Press and was printed and bound in the
United States of America.

Library of Congress Cataloging-in-Publication Data

Blumenberg, Hans.
    [Schiffbruch mit Zuschauer. English]
    Shipwreck with spectator : paradigm of a metaphor for existence / Hans
    Blumenberg ; translated by Steven Rendall.
        p.   cm. — (Studies in contemporary German social thought)
    Includes bibliographical references (p.   ) and index.
    ISBN 978-0-262-51891-8 (pb.:alk. paper)
    1. Philosophy—Miscellanea.   2. Seafaring life in literature.   3. Shipwrecks in
literature.   I. Title.   II. Series.
B68.B5813   1997
193—dc20   96-32034
                                                                            CIP

The MIT Press is pleased to keep this title available in print by
manufacturing single copies, on demand, via digital printing technology.

Vous êtes embarqué
—Pascal

Contents

Translator's Introduction

The publisher's notice printed in the first German edition of *Shipwreck with Spectator* offers a good place to start:

In every culture, what escapes the exertion of the concept—the perspective on the whole of reality, the world, life, and history—is handed over to long-term work on images. The imaginative orientation achieved is condensed, transformed, and elaborated in great metaphors and comparisons. One of the ever-present models is that of life as a sea voyage. It encompasses the voyage out and the voyage home, the harbor and the foreign shore, anchorage and sailing the seas, storm and calm, distress at sea and shipwreck, barely surviving and merely looking on. This metaphor provides the outline of a whole composed of many conditions and possibilities; it also sets the limit of what is nearly impossible, which will, in the best of cases, be recounted as a sailor's yarn.

Shipwreck with Spectator is a study of the seafaring metaphor as a "paradigm," that is, a model open to multiple possible actualizations. By tracing the history of these actualizations, Hans Blumenberg discerns changes in the way human beings have imagined their relation to what the philosopher Edmund Husserl called the *Lebenswelt,* or life-world. He notes that one of the most pervasive actualizations of the life-as-sea-voyage metaphor includes a spectator who observes the distress of those at sea from the safety of dry land. For Blumenberg, this spectator embodies theory (the Greek word *theoría* derives from *theoros*, "spectator") and thus raises the question of what a theoretical perspective on the world entails.

In antiquity, Blumenberg notes, seafaring was seen as a transgression of natural boundaries that was likely to result in punishment. From the outset, then, it was associated with a certain presumption that was not content with the human domain marked out by nature and that sought to go beyond it. "What drives man to cross the high seas is at the same time the crossing of the boundary of his natural needs," Blumenberg observes, and although classical and medieval writers from Hesiod to the Scholastics warned that this transgression exposed men to shipwreck and disaster, "it will be one of the fundamental ideas of the Enlightenment that shipwreck is the price that has to be paid in order that complete calming of the seas not make all worldly commerce impossible."

This appears to parallel the epochal shift Blumenberg outlines in his book *The Legitimacy of the Modern Age*, in which the ancient imperative of self-preservation and the concomitant effort to put the natural world at a distance give way in the Renaissance to "self-assertion" as the project of mastering nature in order to realize human aspirations.[1] This project, like seafaring, is not without risks, but they are risks that modernity is prepared to run. Transgressive passions are compared to the indispensable winds that drive ships across the seas of life but may also drive them onto treacherous shoals. And curiosity, which ancient and medieval thinkers tended to condemn as a desire to know that which we have no natural need to know, is rehabilitated in the modern age:

Voltaire, in fact, justifies the spectator's interest in disasters by reinterpreting it as motivated by intellectual curiosity rather than by pleasure taken in witnessing the sufferings of others.

In a prescient fragment quoted several centuries later by Nietzsche, Pascal had already anticipated the subsequent development of the metaphor when he noted that there is no secure shore from which the spectator may calmly view the distress of those at sea, nor even any question of deciding whether to embark on a perilous voyage. We *are* embarked, Pascal wrote—always already at sea, with no land or harbor in sight. This collapses the protective distance between humankind and nature posited by the ancient metaphor and puts the theoretical perspective itself in jeopardy.

Blumenberg shows that the interrelation, even the identity of the spectator with the object of knowedge, is acknowledged in the writings of nineteenth-century thinkers—philosophers, scientists, historians—and its impact is articulated in terms of the same seafaring metaphor. Amid the shipwreck of scientific theories, the erstwhile spectator is reduced to clinging to a plank, but this bit of debris is precious to him, for it represents his best hope of rebuilding some frail raft that can carry him, if not safely into harbor, at least further on his endless voyage. Yet the prospect of shipwreck looms ever on the horizon, and pursuing the project of human self-assertion in our present situation means being prepared to abandon whatever patched-up craft is currently bearing us across the turbulent seas of existence, in order to leap into the waves and begin, again and again, the task of constructing a new vessel from the materials at hand—including, perhaps, the debris from earlier shipwrecks.

★★★

In the essay that Blumenberg appends to this volume, he reviews the development of studies on metaphor since 1960, when he published his programmatic essay "Paradigms for a Metaphorology."[2] At that time, he says, metaphor was seen as a stage in the process of concept formation, and he envisioned his metaphorology as a "subsidiary method for the history of concepts that was just then emerging." Now, however, the perspective has been reversed: metaphor "is no longer directed mainly toward the constitution of conceptuality but back toward the connections with the life-world as the constant motivating support (though one which cannot be constantly kept in view) of all theory." Whereas metaphorology had earlier focused on the ways in which images mark out the horizon within which concepts are formed, it now focuses on the ways in which they indicate the characteristics of our life-world that lead us to seek theoretical knowledge in the first place. Thus metaphor is currently understood as only one special case of nonconceptuality—that is, of all that in any culture cannot be reduced to concepts.

Blumenberg's reorientation of metaphorology parallels his reorientation of mythology in his *Work on Myth*. As Robert M. Wallace put it in the introduction to his transla-tion of the latter book, "Blumenberg proposes that instead of always interpreting myth in terms of what it (supposedly) came before—its *terminus ad quem*, science, the arrival of which appears to make it obsolete—we should try interpret-ing it in terms of its *terminus a quo*, its point of departure. That point of departure is the problem that myth seeks to solve, which is the source of its real (and lasting) importance, regardless of what (if anything) comes 'after' it."[3] Similarly, in Blumenberg's view, the role of metaphor cannot be adequately understood if it is considered as a mere preliminary to scientific concepts. Not only does it persist in modern discourse, and even in scientific discourse, but it continues to provide the imaginative orientations that constitute the *Lebenswelt*—the all-inclusive horizon of the world as we actually experience it prior to all scientific concepts. *Shipwreck with Spectator* offers a history of the transformations of one such key metaphor.

Finally, a few comments on the translation. Where Blumenberg cites a non-German passage in German translation, I have either substituted a published English translation or retranslated the passage from the original. I have also added English translations of passages Blumenberg cites without giving a German translation. Where feasible, I have provided more complete bibliographical information than the original gives, and occasionally I have substituted references to English translations for Blumenberg's German references. I have omitted a few notes that would be of no interest to English-speaking readers; where I have added notes with interpretive content, I have put them between square brackets and identified them as my own.

Shipwreck with Spectator

1. Seafaring as a Transgression of Boundaries

Humans live their lives and build their institutions on dry land. Nevertheless, they seek to grasp the movement of their existence above all through a metaphorics of the perilous sea voyage. The repertory of this nautical metaphorics of existence is very rich. It includes coasts and islands, harbors and the high seas, reefs and storms, shallows and calms, sail and rudder, helmsmen and anchorages, compass and astronomical navigation, lighthouses and pilots. Often the representation of danger on the high seas serves only to underline the comfort and peace, the safety and serenity of the harbor in which a sea voyage reaches its end. Only where there can be no achievement of a goal, as in the cases of Skeptics and Epicureans, can calm on the high seas itself stand for a vision of pure good fortune.[1]

Among the elementary realities we confront as human beings, the one with which we are least at ease is the sea—with the possible exception of the air, conquered later on. The powers and gods responsible for it stubbornly withdraw from the sphere of determinable forces. Out of the ocean that lies all around the edge of the habitable world come mythical monsters, which are at the farthest remove from the familiar visage of nature and seem to have no knowledge of the world as cosmos. Another feature of this kind of uncanniness is that myth assigns earthquakes—since time immemorial incontestably the most frightening of natural occurrences—to the sea god Poseidon's realm. In the half-mythical explanation given by the first of the Ionian natural philosophers, Thales of Miletus, earthquakes are compared with the swaying of a ship on the sea—and not only metaphorically, since for him the dry land floats on the world ocean.[2] This protophilosopher thereby builds the earliest bridge toward an understanding of the strange paradox from which I began, that human beings living on land nevertheless prefer, in their imagination, to represent their overall condition in the world in terms of a sea voyage.

Two prior assumptions above all determine the burden of meaning carried by the metaphorics of seafaring and shipwreck: first, the sea as a naturally given boundary of the realm of human activities and, second, its demonization as the sphere of the unreckonable and lawless, in which it is difficult to find one's bearings. In Christian iconography as well, the sea is the place where evil appears, sometimes with the Gnostic touch that it stands for all-devouring Matter that takes everything back into itself. It is part of the Johannine apocalypse's promise that, in the messianic fulfillment, there will no longer be a sea (*he thalassa ouk esti eti*). In their purest form, odysseys are an expression of the arbitrariness of the powers that denied Odysseus a homecoming, senselessly driving him about and finally leading him to shipwreck, in which the reliability of the cosmos becomes questionable and its opposite valuation in Gnosticism is anticipated.

The sea has always been suspect for cultural criticism. What could have motivated the move from land to sea but a refusal of nature's meager offerings, the monotony of agricultural labor, plus the addictive vision of quickly won rewards, of more than reason finds necessary (the latter being something the philosophically inclined are always ready to provide a formula for)—the vision, that is, of opulence and luxury? The idea that here, on the boundary between land and sea, what may not have been the *fall* but was certainly a mis*step* into the inappropriate and the immoderate was first taken, has the vividness that sustains lasting topoi.

In his *Works and Days,* Hesiod berates his brother Perses who, with his heart "full of foolishness," has turned away from working on the land toward the opportunity of a sea voyage along the coast, just as their father, "in search of a better life," had often sailed on ships. Hesiod mistrusts the alien element, if only because it is not under the dominion of Zeus—out on the high seas, earthshaker Poseidon acts in accord with his own decisions. For that reason, he advises Perses not to stay beyond the lawful boundaries of the favorable season and to return home as fast as he can. The rules of time seem to be what remain of the cosmos for the sea. For this reason, Hesiod strongly criticizes sea voyages under the uncertain conditions of spring; they are "hasty and audacious." Yet humans, "with their hearts' lack of understanding," do set out on such voyages.

It is precisely in this criticism that we first encounter the culture-critical connection between two elements characterized by liquidity: water and money. The latter is said to be "like life itself to pitiable mankind."[3] This tool of the absolute interchange of all with all creates out of the separation of peoples, which is considered to be in accord

---

with nature, the unmarked road by which they can be connected. In keeping with the schema that is established in advance here, Virgil, less apocalyptic than the prophet John, foresees in his fourth *Eclogue* the end, not indeed of the sea, but of seafaring, in the coming age of bliss.

2. What the Shipwrecked Person Is Left With

In this field of representation, shipwreck is something like the "legitimate" result of seafaring, and a happily reached harbor or serene calm on the sea is only the deceptive face of something that is deeply problematic. The contraposition of dry land and deep sea as the primary frame of reference for the paradoxical metaphorics of existence might, however, lead us to expect that, going beyond the ideas of storms at sea and sinkings, there must also be the, as it were, emphatic configuration in which shipwreck at sea is set beside the uninvolved spectator on dry land. One is inclined to say a priori that this convergence could hardly fail to occur in literature; it could also hardly fail to scandalize if it presents the uninvolved spectator as the type who, culture-critically or even aesthetically, takes note of his distance[4] from the enormity [*das Ungemässe*] with satisfaction or even enjoyment. The proem to the second book of Lucretius's didactic poem, together with its reception history, will lead us in this direction.

Before that, we should examine more closely the ancient suspicion that underlies the metaphorics of shipwreck: that there is a frivolous, if not blasphemous, moment inherent in all human seafaring, on a par with an offense against the invulnerability of the earth, the law of *terra inviolata*, which seemed to forbid cutting through isthmuses or building artificial harbors—in other words, radical alterations of the relationship between land and sea. In the writings of ancient historians, there are still references both to respecting and to flouting this law. But prohibitions have always also defined the extreme limits of daring and challenge.[5]

Horace introduced the "ship of state" into political rhetoric, where it plays its role down to the present day.[6] However, the resolution—correctly described as allegorical—of the problem posed by Ode 1.4, in which Quintilian takes the ship as the state (*navem pro re publica*) and interprets the storms as civil wars, is not beyond doubt. The poet sees the ship dashed under by storms from the point of view of the lamenting but uninvolved spectator. Quintilian's decoding was authoritative for the way this metaphor was handed down, and it was also made habitual by an established form going back to Alcaeus.[7] But the ode's ship, in its thoughtfully observed pitiable state, is also in accord with the warning about seafaring that Horace gave in his *Proemptikon* (sent along with Virgil on his voyage to Athens), which is among the most common citations from him. He speaks expressly of forbidden voyages over the sea and of ships as "impious boats" (*inpiae rates*)[8] that rashly connect what a divinity has sundered. When the sea throws itself against the fragile vessel, it is only protecting this original division established by the gods' wisdom and overleaped by human pride:

Audax omnia perpeti
Gens humana ruit per vetitum nefas . . . .[9]

Horace compares such an offense with that of Prometheus, who also seized by force an alien element not allowed to men. Daedalus represents the third element forbidden to men. Flying through the air, seafaring, and stealing fire are brought together in one context. Folly seems here already to be storming the heights of heaven, and God is within his rights in hurling his wrathful thunderbolts against it. The element that is omitted is the earth; the interpolated thought is that solid ground is the appropriate place for men to live.

Shipwreck, as seen by a survivor, is the figure of an initial philosophical experience. It is said that the founder of the Stoic school, Zeno of Cition, was shipwrecked with a cargo of Phoenician purple dye near Piraeus and was led thereby to philosophy, summing up: *nyn euploeka, hote nenauageka*— "I was first fortunate in seafaring when I was shipwrecked."[10] Vitruvius reports that the Socratic philosopher Aristippus, shipwrecked on the shores of the island of Rhodes, recognized that there were humans nearby when he saw geometrical figures traced on the beach. The account has the philosopher—who was not exactly esteemed by the other students of Socrates, because he was too well acquainted with money and pleasure—undergo a kind of conversion. He entrusted to his homebound fellow passengers the message that one ought to provide one's children with only such possessions as could be saved from a shipwreck (*quae e naufragio una possent enatare*), for the only things important in life were those that neither the trials of fate nor revolution nor war could harm.[11] We have here the moralizing version of an anecdote that originally related to sophistic practice: even in the hopeless situation of being shipwrecked on a foreign shore, a philosophically trained person still knows what to do, when he recognizes civilized reason in geometrical diagrams and thereupon decides to proceed immediately to the city's gymnasium and earn through philosophical disputation what he needs to restore his lost outfit.

That is, he is a man who can take care of himself rather than a man who draws lessons from the shipwreck. This is the slick sales promotion for sophistic teaching, whose profitability was the source of Aristippus's poor reputation among the Socratics. In the list of Aristippus's lost dialogues given by Diogenes Laertius, we find listed second the title "To Shipwrecked Men."[12]

In early May 1539, when Joachim Rhetikus left his recently assumed chair of mathematics in Wittenberg in order to seek out, in remotest Prussia, the reformer of astronomy who was then known only through rumors and to study his doctrine first-hand, it seemed to him that this trip to Frauenburg was prefigured by Aristippus's shipwreck. In his "First Report," which appeared in Danzig in 1540 and disseminated the first authentic information about Copernicus's theory, Rhetikus writes about the mathematician's special gain in familiarity on the foreign shore: "The shipwreck Aristippus is supposed to have suffered on the island of Rhodes is often cited: when the man whom the sea had just thrown up on the land espied geometrical figures on the beach, he encouraged his fellow passengers by calling out that he saw traces of men. He was not mistaken in this assumption, for through his wealth of knowledge he easily persuaded the learned and virtuous inhabitants to provide him and his companions with everything they needed to live. Now, Prussians eagerly welcome guests, but by God I have so far entered scarcely any reputable man's house in this country without already finding geometrical figures on the threshold, or perceiving that the love of geometry is for them a spiritual need."

The Göttingen mathematician Abraham Gotthelf Kästner, in his 1759 essay "On the Value of Mathematics, Considered as a Pastime," paid less attention to the stranded philosopher in the shipwreck anecdote than to the unknown person whose interest in geometry had resulted in the figures in the sand, thereby supposedly supplying a proof for Kästner's proposition: "In this world there is no place so barren that those who understand mathematics will not be employed in measuring dimensions, figures, forces. . . . A sandy beach allowed the geometer of Rhodes at least to sketch some figures, and thereby to reveal to the shipwrecked philosopher that human beings lived there."[13]

The classical advice to conduct one's life in such a way as to limit one's traveling needs to what can be carried along by a shipwrecked man swimming for the shore is attributed by Diogenes Laertius to another Socratic, Antisthenes. It almost goes without saying that Montaigne did not let this saying escape him; in the essay "Of Solitude," he drew from it a new point in favor of moral autarky. He cites it verbatim from Diogenes and then gives it his unmistakable twist: "Certainly a man of understanding has lost nothing, if he has himself."[14] What can be salvaged from the shipwreck of existence proves to be not a possession withdrawn, in whatever way, into interiority but rather the self-possession achievable through the process of self-discovery and self-appropriation. Long before it divests itself of the security of its relationship to the world, skeptical anthropology defines as its property what it can allow as a substance that is not endangered and cannot be lost. To the outside that cannot be reached from the inside corresponds—and in this Montaigne already moves close to Descartes—the inside that cannot be reached from the outside.

But for the skeptic, too, the ultimate is always still before him. The test of the reliability of the substance he has discovered ends only when his life ends. True, he can thank his good fortune that he has thus far not been burdened by greater suffering than he could bear. "Might it not be Fortune's way to leave in peace those who do not trouble her?"[15] There, however, the shipwreck metaphor chimes in at the last minute like a warning bell: "But beware the crash. There are thousands who are wrecked in port."[16] The image of the sea voyage that can still come to grief in the harbor intersects in Montaigne's nautical metaphorics with another one: "I cling to what I see and hold, and do not go far from port."[17] This corresponds more or less to his other metaphor, which warns us not to swim against the current in the conduct of our lives.

For Montaigne, leaving port also means abandoning oneself wholly to the optical subjectivity he discovered in Virgil's line *Provehimur portu, terraeque urbesque recedunt* ("We leave the port, and lands and towns retreat").[18] What does the interpretation of this image in terms of optical subjectivity vouch for? Montaigne speaks of death and of the delusion of the dying man who refuses to believe that this, in particular, must be his last hour. The delusive hope is founded on our placing "too much importance on ourselves."[19] Montaigne suggests that we cannot imagine that things go on unaffected without us, that they do not suffer through our departure. Just as it seems to seafarers that mountains, fields, cities, the sky and the earth draw away as they themselves move away from the land, so "our vision, when altered, represents things to itself as being likewise altered, and we think they are failing it in proportion as it is failing them."[20] On the high seas of optical subjectivity, there is only one rule, which once again resembles Descartes's "provisional morality": in any case, hold a steady course.[21]

Even if private existence escapes shipwreck from inner perils, there still remain the great sinkings of the state, of the world, that can take it down along with them. Montaigne gave the metaphor its most sweeping form in connection with the story of Atticus reported by Cornelius Nepos, when he allows Atticus, through his moderation, to save himself from the "universal shipwreck of the world."[22] Montaigne himself espouses "the general and just cause" only with moderation, and he will go down with it only if necessity gives him no other choice; otherwise, he will let himself be rescued. By whom? By himself—for in this one case, he speaks of himself in the double role of savior and saved, referring to himself as "Montaigne": "Let Montaigne be engulfed in the public ruin, if need be; but if not, I shall be grateful to fortune if he is saved; and as much rope as my duty gives me, I use for his preservation."[23] One can almost feel how the skeptic approaches the secure position of the spectator, by raising higher and higher the conditions under which he would still be prepared to allow himself to go down, in what was then a thirty-year-old political situation. When reading historians, Montaigne tells us, he nevertheless always deplores the fact that he has not witnessed the confusions of other nations. His curiosity leads him frankly to consider it an asset that he has seen with his own eyes the drama of the national catastrophe ("this notable spectacle of our public death"), its symptoms, and its form; since he could not prevent it, he is glad he was destined to be its spectator. The inescapable comparison with tragedy in the theater follows immediately: "Not that we lack compassion for what we see and hear; but the exceptional nature of these pathetic events arouses a pain that gives us pleasure."[24] Here, an author like Montaigne would be unable to resist quoting Lucretius on shipwreck and the spectator. But he has already "used" this quotation to another end. Instead of employing it to describe his position as contrasted with the great spectacle of the state, he has adduced it as evidence for the paradoxical assertion that nothing in nature is useless, even uselessness (*inutilité*).[25]

According to Montaigne's argument, human entities are held together by pathological qualities: ambition, jealousy, envy, vengeance, superstition, despair, and even cruelty. Compassion itself is adulterated with a sort of bittersweet feeling of malicious pleasure. Montaigne claims that this is a property of human nature and not merely a corruption of adults, noting that even children feel this way. And he immediately cites the first two lines of the Proem to Book 2 of Lucretius's *De Rerum Natura*. These lines are explained only by the assertion that the fundamental preconditions of our life would be destroyed if we were to try to root out these questionable qualities in men. Montaigne does not justify the spectator of shipwreck by his right to enjoyment; rather, he justifies his pleasure, positively described as malicious (*volupté maligne*), by his successful self-preservation. By virtue of his capacity for this distance, he stands unimperiled on the solid ground of the shore. He survives through one of his useless qualities: the ability to be a spectator. The spectator's enjoyment no longer has the existential success it had in ancient theory, where it led to happiness (*eudaemonia*) as the pure form of the relationship to the world. Rather, its comfort is something like the cunning of nature, in that it sets a premium on taking as little risk as possible with one's life and rewards distance with enjoyment.

But here, in order to complete my discussion of Montaigne the metaphorist, I have hastened prematurely to the reception of Lucretius. First, we must pursue further the image of the shipwrecked man who, on the strength of his self-possession alone, comes out of the catastrophe unharmed.

One of those who know something about making their way through catastrophes in one piece is Goethe. Speaking in 1809 to the Hamburg diplomat Carl Sieveking, he referred to his happy youth, remarking that the world "has become more serious" since that time: "then one would have been allowed to lose years, now not a single day." This is, taken in itself, an older man's remark, valid for every process of aging as a formula for the preciousness of time. However, it then becomes clear that this act of economy, which nature imposes on us, is bound up with another constraint, originating in the historical situation: "like the shipwrecked, we must hold tight to the plank that saved us, and put our precious lost baggage out of our minds."[26]

It is also worth noting the connection Goethe establishes between the lack of success of his color theory and the metaphorics of shipwreck. A statement from 1830 allows us to see that saving plank, conjured up two decades earlier, and the loneliness of the man who is saved, for whom alone the plank has room, in the light of a disappointment with life. To Soret, the Genevese tutor of the Weimar princes, Goethe speaks of his traumatic experience, of the resistances and prejudices against his theory of colors, which apparently allows no more than *one man* to be favored by its truth: "it is as if in a great shipwreck one were able to seize a saving plank sufficient to carry one man, and were saved all alone, the rest of the passengers wretchedly drowning."[27]

The twist Nietzsche gave to nautical metaphorics, and which people might at times have liked to call "existential," was discovered by Pascal in the formula "you are embarked." It occurs in the *pensée* that develops the wager argument. Whoever is still hesitating to wager the whole finite stake in the hope of an infinite reward is supposed thereby to be persuaded that the game has already begun, the stake is already on the table, and all that remains is to perceive the whole infinity of chance. The skeptic's abstention, which Montaigne had expressed through the image of remaining in the harbor, is in Pascal's view not an option. The metaphorics of embarkation includes the suggestion that living means already being on the high seas, where there is no outcome other than being saved or going down, and no possibility of abstention. Pascal, whom Nietzsche for this reason saw as the "only logical Christian," excluded the thought of simple self-preservation, which does not seek the absolute raising of the stake, the infinite gain. Only thus could this "most instructive victim of Christianity" antici- pate Nietzsche, who follows Pascal almost verbatim with this thought: "We have left the land and have embarked. We have burned our bridges behind us—indeed, we have gone further and destroyed the land behind us. Now, little ship, look out! . . . and there is no longer any 'land.'"[28] Over this fragment taken from the *Gay Science* is written, as if to remind us of Pascal, "*In the horizon of the infinite.*"

The next metaphorical step is that not only are we always already embarked and on the high seas but also, as if this were inevitable, we are shipwrecked. It goes almost without saying that, in the complex of notes to the completed parts of Nietzsche's *Zarathustra,* we find the shipwreck scene. The fragment entitled "On turmoil" reads: "Once, when Zarathustra as the result of a shipwreck was spat out upon the land and rode on a wave, he said in wonder: 'Where is my fate now? I do not know where I should go. I am losing myself.' He threw himself into the turmoil. Then, overcome by disgust, he sought some consolation—himself."[29] It is the almost "natural" permanent condition of life, which the

Prince de Ligne had first expressed (in 1759, in a letter to his former tutor de la Porte) by means of a comparison with shipwreck: "You have taught me everything, except swimming, and Calypso and Eucharis, in an attack of indignation, would certainly have thrown me into the sea. Out of fear of avoiding even a single shipwreck, I have not avoided a single reef, but I have never gone under, because I have always saved myself by means of some plank, and I am very content, at that."[30] This, too, is an epigonic form of the ancient *ataraxia*: shipwreck sought out and demanded, as a test of an unbreakable well-being. This procedure, not avoiding a single reef, will later be called "heroic nihilism."

In one of Nietzsche's plans from 1875 is found the outline of an "ironic novella" on the theme "everything is false," with the note "How man clings to a beam."[31] Notice that this is not the familiar metaphor according to which man grasps at straws, whose defect is that they are not durable. There the initial situation is unknown, and only the momentary weakness is registered. In the case of Nietzsche's beam, the shipwreck is in the background, no longer has to be made explicit, and turns everything into an instrument of naked self-preservation. It is what remains after a sinking in which the artificial vehicle of self-deception and self-assurance was long since smashed to pieces: "For the liberated intellect, that enormous timber and framework of concepts, clinging to which needy humankind saves itself for life, is only a scaffolding and a toy for his boldest works of art: and if he smashes it, mixes it up, and ironically puts it back together, pairing what is most alien and separating what is most closely related, he shows that he does not need these forms of emergency assistance."[32]

It was his friend Franz Overbeck who saw Nietzsche and his thought in the perspective of the shipwreck metaphor, and not only when his madness had set in. "Desperation seized him during his voyage," Overbeck suggested, "and he abandoned his vessel itself." But no one had yet reached the goal of this voyage, and "in that measure Nietzsche failed no more than anyone else." His smash-up can therefore no more be used as an argument against the voyage he undertook than a shipwreck can be used as an argument against seafaring. "Just as someone who has reached a harbor will least of all refuse to recognize his shipwrecked predecessor as a fellow-sufferer, so also more fortunate seafarers who have at least been able to hold their own with a vessel, on their aimless voyage, will do the same with respect to Nietzsche."[33] It was no accident that Overbeck spoke this language and found these images, for he was also, as a theologian, the rediscoverer of the apocalyptic tenor in the New Testament and the discoverer of the self-destruction of every theology that is based on eschatological expectation, a man whose legacy bore the title "Last Theology"—and whose final concern was to have it burned.

Nietzsche himself carried the imagination of seafaring and shipwreck even a few steps further. Those rescued from shipwreck are astonished by their new experience of dry land. This is the fundamental experience of science, that it is able to establish things that stand firm and provide solid ground for further discoveries. It could have been otherwise, as is shown by other ages' belief in fantastic metamorphoses and marvels. The reliability of firm ground is something wholly new for humans who are surfacing out of history. Nietzsche compares what he calls his happiness to that of the shipwrecked man who has "climbed ashore, and now stands with both feet on the firm old earth—amazed that it does not rock."[34] Terra firma is not the position of the spectator but rather that of the man rescued from shipwreck; its firmness is experienced wholly out of the sense of the unlikelihood that such a thing should be attainable at all.

Nietzsche undertook his other broadening of the metaphor of the inevitable and irreversible sea voyage by referring to the "new world" not, indeed, as the goal but as the reward of the risk undertaken. The elation of his stay in Genoa, which lasted until spring 1882, is expressed through identification with the Genoese Columbus. In the fragment "Embark!" in *The Gay Science,* he transforms Columbus's reflections as he was setting out to discover a new world into a call to philosophers to set out: "The moral earth, too, is round. . . . There is another world to be discovered—and more than one. Embark, philosophers!"[35] During the winter in Genoa, Nietzsche was already pondering great gestures of rebirth, world adventures, the foundation of colonies, and even war—all as "the compulsion to participate in the smallest way in a great sacrifice." The result was that, using a made-up pretext, he persuaded the captain of a Sicilian sailing freighter to let him go along to Messina as the sole passenger. The adventure lasted exactly four days. The weather was good, and he came nowhere near shipwreck. Thus was produced "The New Columbus," a transformation of "Toward New Seas," but still lacking the second stanza with its doubtful line "Before me sea—and land? And land?" which was inserted only two years later into a poem addressed to Lou Salomé ("Friend, said Columbus, trust/No one from Genoa again!").[36]

Through the mood he experienced during the days he spent on the sailing ship between Genoa and Messina, Nietzsche believed he had understood the Greek Epicurus. In *The Gay Science,* he declares his pride at having attained a unique sympathy with the character of Epicurus. He believes he can thereby enjoy "the happiness of the after-noon of antiquity" in a way that only "someone who suffered continually" could have discovered. It is the "happiness of eyes that have seen the sea of existence become calm."[37] This, too, is the happiness of a spectator but not that of the Epicurean Lucretius, whose scene of emergency at sea, with its onlooker, Nietzsche wholly neglects in his thinking, regarding it as alien to the Greek. It is not the sea's calm and serenity that gratify the spectator, by way of his eyes; rather, wholly in the style of the idealistic subject, it is the power of the sufferer, the happiness of his eyes, before which a metaphorical "sea of existence" has *become calm*. The metaphor is a projection, a mastering anthropomorphizing of nature in the service of the subject, who is reflected in it. Here Nietzsche has brought the Greek completely under his power.

In this passage, we find the profound observation that the image type of the "shipwreck with spectator" would have been far from the thoughts of a Greek. If this could be verified, the best evidence would be the often-cited and puzzled-over distich by an anonymous Greek poet, who not only greets the finally reached harbor and bids farewell to hope and chance but also calls on the personified *Spes* and *Fortuna* (Hope and Fortune) to continue with others the game it has finished with the one who has reached land: "I have found the port. Farewell, Hope and Fortune!/You have played enough with me. Now play with other men!" (*Inveni portum. Spes et fortuna valete!/ Sat me lusistis. Ludite nunc alios!*). This is only one of the various Latin versions into which this poem from the *Anthologia Palatina*,[38] a collection put together shortly before the end of the first millennium, was transformed. Anselm Feuerbach uses this version in

1814 when, having been driven from Munich by intrigues and promoted by his king to a high judge's office in Bamberg, he concludes his thanks to the monarch, with ironic resignation, with the distich. Here the apotropaic request that the treacherous powers of life play with other men is hardly important.

The Venetian adventurer Casanova alone attributes the distich to Euripides. The familiar Aristotelian theory of tragic catharsis may have led Casanova to make this attribution. These verses were recommended to him by the abbot of Einsiedeln as a cell motto when the abbot was about to admit the allegedly converted sinner into his cloister. The abbot had heard Casanova's confession two weeks earlier, and he knew what he was offering this man with *spes et fortuna valete*. Casanova had already sinned again, however, not having been able to resist the beauty from Solothurn. In the beginning of this conversion, from which he quickly recovered, he had been spontaneously tempted, at the epicurean abbot's sumptuous table, to decide to request admission to the cloister: "I believed I had recognized that here was the place where I could happily live until my last hour, without offering fate the slightest opening for an attack."[39] The abbot's motto thus hits the mark insofar as it comprehends Casanova's thoughts of death and age, which form the underlying obligato theme of *The History of My Life*—the melancholy that governs throughout all its adventures. Still, the pagan concluding twist, passing on to others the game from which he wants to escape, has no attraction for Casanova. His memoirs prove that, even in the recollections of his actual old age, he wished only to enjoy once again his own life, and that the lives of others, including those who were also entangled in his game, had always been a matter of indifference to him.

Gil Blas de Santillana, the hero of Lesage's picaresque novel, dreams in prison of buying a cottage in the country, after he is freed, and living there as a philosopher. His wish is granted beyond his expectations; his former master, who has in the interim become, not without Gil's collaboration, the governor of Valencia, gives him the little estate of Liria, with these words that are quite appropriate in the philosophical tradition and still define the ending of Voltaire's *Candide*: "Henceforth you are no longer to be Fortune's plaything; I want to shelter you from its power and make you master of a property that it may not steal away from you." Gil refuses a yearly pension, because he considers riches to be only a burden in a restful retreat where one seeks nothing but peace. It is true that his final taking possession of the little castle is still three books away, but the inscription that is to be put in golden letters over the door has already been settled at the end of the tenth book: it is the harbor distich in its most common variant, the first one I cited above.[40] Just as Casanova, the adventurer who oscillates between resignation and new attractions, thinks only of enjoying his own memories in old age, but has already ironically surpassed the distich as soon as it crops up, so the hero of the picaresque novel is completely unsuited to the refined, distanced enjoyment of watching fate play with other people. He dreams naively of a cottage and receives a small castle; being able to say farewell to being battered about the world is the sum total of his wishes.

It is true that the distich's reception history does not tell us what would have distinguished it from images like Lucretius's, but it does tell us how it was suited to leaving the spectator's distance out of account, even as a possibility, when another kind of life fulfillment is offered. The element of security in the harbor eliminates the possibility of a Caspar

David Friedrich point of view, high above the surging (fog)sea, as the undisturbed and reflective observer of other people's shipwrecks.

3. Aesthetics and Ethics of the Spectator

The pattern was set by the Roman, Lucretius. At the beginning of the second book of his cosmic poem, he imagines observing, from the safety of shore, other people who are in peril on the storm-tossed sea: "e terra magnum alterius spectare laborem." Clearly, the pleasantness that is said to characterize this sight is not a result of seeing someone else suffer but of enjoying the safety of one's own standpoint. It has nothing to do with a relationship among men, between those who suffer and those who do not; it has rather to do with the relationship between philosophers and reality; it has to do with the advantage gained through Epicurus's philosophy, the possession of an inviolable, solid ground for one's view of the world. Even the spectator of mighty battles who is not threatened by the perils of war has to be aware of the difference between the need for happiness and the ruthless caprice of physical reality. Only the observer who is secured by philosophy can blunt this difference into a distance. It is the sage—or at least the man who is prepared for the natural process and the business of the world by the *doctrina sapientum*—who both carries the theory ideal of classical Greek philosophy, figured by the spectator, through to its end and contradicts it on a decisive point.

The contradiction consists in this: what the spectator enjoys is not the sublimity of the objects his theory opens up for him but his own self-consciousness, over against the whirl of atoms out of which everything that he observes is constituted, including himself. The cosmos is no longer the Order whose contemplation fills the observer with happiness (*Eudaemonia*). It is at most the remaining assurance that such a firm ground exists at all, beyond the reach of the hostile element. To this extent, it is important not only that Epicurus is a Greek and Lucretius a Roman but perhaps still more that two centuries separate them. The indifference of theory has made itself into the equivalent, in rank and power, of reality's indifference to man, its constituent part.

In the same way, Epicurus and Lucretius embodied in the sage himself something of the image of their gods, who had, as it were, passed through philosophy to their situation outside the worlds. The gods can be happy, as they are said to be, only because they are neither the authors nor the administrators of what happens in the world and are concerned wholly with themselves. The spectator of the world cannot be so pure. He needs at least the physics of the atoms to consolidate his own modest existence almost outside the world. Only God could be a true spectator, and he has no interest in this role. Nevertheless, the late Middle Ages— forgetting Aristotle's doctrine of the exclusiveness of the unmoved mover's self-preoccupation—made God as well into a spectator of the theater of the world. As if God had interrupted his eternity only for that purpose, all creatures become for him, as Luther put it, "masks and mummers" in a "game of God's, who has allowed them to exalt themselves a little bit."

When Lucretius resorts once again to the metaphor of distress at sea and of shipwreck, he accordingly speaks of his universe of randomly moving atoms as an ocean of matter (*pelagus materiae*), from which the forms of nature are thrown onto the beach of visible appearance, like the debris from a massive shipwreck (*quasi naufragiis magnis multisque coortis*), as a warning to mortals of the perils of the sea. It is only because the supply of atoms is inexhaustible that the catastrophes of physical reality continue to be fruitful in forms and to allow the man standing on the shore of appearance to observe a certain regularity. One sees what the *indicium mortalibus* (advice to mortals) means here: man does well to be content with the spectator's role and not to abandon his philosophical standpoint before and above the natural world. As an individual, he can gain no advantage from the identity of catastrophe and productivity in this theory of an ever-developing, ever-dissolving universe.[41]

In the great cultural critique in Book 5, Lucretius resorts once more to the nautical metaphorics. As in Book 2, in which all bringing forth of natural forms was seen in terms of shipwreck, here the birth of man is seen in the same way.[42] Nature takes the child from the mother's body and throws it on the shores of light (*in luminis oras*), just as the raging waves hurl the sailor onto land. Not only the course of life and its end are seen through the shipwreck metaphor, but even its beginning. Here, too, the representation of seafaring as unnatural is in the background, in a still sharper culture-critical form. Primitive man, living within his natural limits, knew seafaring as little as he knew death by thousands in battle *sub signis*. The man who was content with his meager existence was tempted in vain by the sea to make the misstep of culture: "the wicked art of navigation then lay hidden and obscure" (*inproba navigii ratio tum caeca iacebat*).[43]

The metaphorical and the real events of transgressing the boundary between terra firma and the sea beyond blend into each other, like the metaphorical and the real risks of shipwreck. What drives man to cross the high seas is at the same time what drives him to go beyond the boundary of his natural needs. Thus, the human race struggles fruitlessly and in vain, consuming its life in futile cares, because it does not stop at the goal and limit of possession and does not even know how far genuine pleasure can be further increased. The same attraction that gradually leads life to venture out to sea also leads to the outbreak of wars.[44] The crime of seafaring punishes itself through the fear of mighty powers to which man subjects himself, and which he translates into the images of his gods, for whom these powers stand in.[45] That he cannot ally himself with such powers he sees immediately through the futility of his efforts to win them over—"all in vain, for he is nonetheless often driven by the powerful hurricane into the depths of death."

In complete contrast to this, it will be one of the fundamental ideas of the Enlightenment that shipwreck is the price that must be paid in order to avoid that complete calming of the sea winds that would make all worldly commerce impossible. Through this figure is expressed a justification of the *passiones*, the passions, against which philosophy discriminates: pure reason would mean the absence of winds and the motionlessness of human beings who possess complete presence of mind.

In one of his *Dialogues of the Dead,* modeled on Lucian, Fontenelle has Herostratus, the man who burned down the temple at Ephesus, argue with Demetrius of Phalerum about whether one ought to be able to gain fame both by building and by destroying. The one had sought fame by having 360 statues erected in Athens; the other had reduced the temple of Ephesus to ashes. Herostratus defends destruction by means of the paradox that it alone gives men the room to make themselves eternal: "The earth is like a large tablet, on which each man wish〰 ɔo write his name. When it becomes full, then the names already written there have to be erased, in order to put new ones in their place. What would happen if all the monuments of the ancients were still standing?" The vengeful passion that makes one man destroy the statues and buildings another erects is at the same time a desire to clear away impediments to new initiatives and rationality. Herostratus is able to put an end to this debate in the underworld by observing, "The inclinations of the soul make and destroy everything. If reason reigned over the earth, nothing would happen on it. It is said that sailors fear most of all calm seas and that they want wind, even at the risk of tempests. In men, passions are the winds that are necessary to put everything in movement, even if they sometimes cause storms and turbulence."

This sort of setting off of the powers of the world against each other becomes common in the Enlightenment; shipwreck as an ultimate possibility is not expressly mentioned. The fact that being shattered and sunk by shipwreck can be an unheroic model is discussed in another of Fontenelle's dialogues, which brings together the Roman emperor Hadrian and Margaret of Austria, the daughter of Maximilian ("last of the knights") and Mary of Burgundy. The emperor would like to measure his death against the model provided by Cato of Utica; Margaret objects that there is nothing easier than dying if one goes about it in the right way. Hadrian wants to be able to see the way he died, which had nothing unusual about it (he died in bed, peacefully and without notice, but not without leaving behind a cheerful little poem), as having the form honored by philosophy: it is characterized by ease rather than defiance. Margaret, however, thinks she can offer something better—more beauty, less audience.

According to her account, she was on her way by sea to join her future husband, Philibert II of Savoy, when a storm put her in danger of shipwreck and she took the opportunity to think out her epitaph. Her death by shipwreck moves completely in the realm of fiction, of anticipation, but it is supposed, precisely for that reason, to characterize a cheerful composure, midway between Cato's defiance and Hadrian's frivolity: "To tell the truth, I did not die that time, but I was helpless to prevent it. . . . Cato's steadfastness is too extreme in one way, and yours too extreme in the other; but mine is natural. He is too forced, and you are too amusing, but I am reasonable."

Margaret regards the cold-bloodedness of the two ancient philosophers as suspect: there can be violence in a poem as well as in a dagger. The threat of shipwreck was, by contrast, entirely external violence without staging. In such a situation, it means something to compose one's epitaph calmly, with sangfroid. "All your lives, you were both very preoccupied with being philosophers, and thus you had undertaken not to fear death. . . . I, on the other hand, had every right to tremble and quake during this prolonged storm, and to scream to high heaven, without anyone being able to blame me or make the slightest objection; my honor would not have been in the least damaged thereby. However, I remained so calm that I was able to compose an epitaph for myself."

At this point in the contest between the two shades to determine who had the most meaningful death, the emperor becomes indiscreet and asks whether this famous epitaph was not composed afterward, once Margaret was back on dry land: "Entre nous, l'épitaphe ne fût-elle point faite sur la terre?" Margaret responds to this intrusive probing of the true conditions under which she composed her epitaph with a counterquestion: can she expect the emperor also to reveal the origin of his famous poem? She can be referring only to the verses (included in the *Anthologia Palatina*) in which Hadrian addresses his own soul as the guest and companion of the body and, in dying, bids it farewell: "*Animula, vagula, blandula / Hospes comesque corporis, / Quae nunc abibis in loca / Pallidula, rigida, nudula, / Nec, ut soles, dabis iocos.*"[46] Margaret does not even ask the emperor's shade whether one speaks in this way while dying or only while toying with the thought of death. So he has to agree that everyday norms are adequate, including moderation even in virtue, which "is great enough, when it does not go beyond the bounds of nature." This is a formula of resignation for two spectators of death and shipwreck who watch from the safe shore—the shore of the underworld, where the dead are beyond the reach of catastrophe. This metaphysically exaggerated distance from earthly disasters, with its postexistent "wisdom," is ironic, as is its rejection of the insinuation that the poetic triumph over the critical instance could in either case have been invented in advance, or only afterward, and thus remained an "existentially" unactualized aesthetic attitude.

A novel variety of the shipwreck metaphor, one found only in the modern epoch, is first produced by the Enlightenment's cosmic exoticism, of which Fontenelle, again, was one of the inventors. Its fundamental idea was that reason might be better represented on the moon or in another alien world than it is on earth and by men. The imagination was then bound to be continually stimulated to picture how the earth would be seen from the point of view of such a higher rationality. Voltaire was to do this in *Micromégas*, but Fontenelle beat him to it and provided the pattern of a witty reversal of perspective.

In Fontenelle's *Conversations on the Plurality of Worlds* the marquise, the prototype of the female with a thirst for knowledge and enlightenment who recurs in many Enlightenment treatises, receives her elementary instruction in astronomy and speculative cosmology. This courtly philosophical text was read well into the nineteenth century. Among the many subjects proposed for reflection in it are the difficulties that curious moon inhabitants would encounter during a visit to the earth. The earthly atmosphere is as heavy and thick in comparison with that of the moon as water is in comparison with air; thus, lunar astronauts coming into our atmosphere would drown and fall dead onto the earth. Confronted with this possibility, the marquise's curiosity plunges on: "Oh, how I wish some great shipwreck would occur that scattered a lot of those people here, so that we could easily go look at their extraordinary shapes!"[47] But the philosopher must also warn her about these beings of loftier origin, for one must always be aware that they may be able to reverse the relationship of spectator and object. The lunar voyagers could do this very easily "if they were clever enough to sail along the outer layer of our air, and thus look down on us out of curiosity, angling for us like fish." It is characteristic of the theoretical audacity of the newly invented female Enlightenment character that the marquise does not shy away from this risk either; as an object, she is still at least to some degree a spectator, and she might go willingly into the alien fishermen's net, "just to have the pleasure of seeing the beings that had caught me." The Enlightenment philosopher, finding himself unexpectedly forced to calm his pupil's curiosity, must enter into an elaborate argument to talk her out of this.

Voltaire generates further variations on this successful paradigm in his story about a traveler to other worlds. He is not as original in this as in his decisive contradiction of Lucretius's configuration. Against the latter, he summons up the full pathos of his moral philosophy. He must, however, accept shipwreck as a given, because for Voltaire, too, "passions" are the energy that puts the human world in motion. Cultivating one's garden in the withdrawal of resignation, as Candide does at the end of his adventures, cannot be represented as the wisdom of the beginning, like Epicurus's philosophical existence turned away from the world in his "garden." Candide, too, must live through his shipwreck near Lisbon, see the righteous Anabaptist sink into the sea while the brutal sailor survives, so that his resignation at the end might not be eaten away by the "passion" of believing that something in the world might have escaped him. Voltaire does not trust renunciations of the world.

Zadig, the hero of Voltaire's earliest philosophical tale about the absence of freedom, complains to a hermit about how disastrous human passions are. The hermit replies that they are like the wind that fills the sail of a ship, which, although it sometimes capsizes the ship, is also responsible for its moving at all. It is like gall, which can make us choleric and ill but without which we cannot live. This life is in fact kept going only by means of things that can also be fatal to it: *Tout est dangereux ici-bas, et tout est nécessaire.*[48] Shipwreck is only a symptom of this antinomy of moving force and threat.

For this reason, Montaigne's advice not to leave the harbor for the sea is no longer feasible. The Marquise du Châtelet, Voltaire's worldly-wise and learned friend at the castle of Cirey, in her treatise "On Happiness" (first published in 1779, thirty years after her death), makes lingering in the harbor of rational deliberation responsible for the loss of any opportunity to win happiness in life. Once again, it is one of the antinomies of human existence that reflection and projection must precede the action, so that one can become happy, but this postpones the actualization so long that once we know how to reach the goal, other obstacles have already blocked the way to it. "Prévenons ces réflexions qu'on fait plus tard." Thus she begins her treatise by counseling the reader not to waste on deliberation part of the precious, brief time we have to feel and think—not to spend time caulking the ship when he could already be at sea, enjoying the pleasures to be found there.[49] The harbor is not an alternative to shipwreck; it is the site where the pleasures of life are foregone.

However, the spectator, too, no longer represents the exceptional existence of the sage, on the edge of reality; rather, he has himself become an exponent of one of those passions that both move and endanger life. It is true that he is not personally involved in adventures, but he certainly is helplessly at the mercy of the attraction of catastrophes and sensations. His noninvolvement is not that of looking on but that of a burning curiosity. What Voltaire refuses to grant to Lucretius (whose lines in the Proem he quotes at least twice) is the spectator's reflectiveness with respect to other people's imperilment at sea. That human beings hurry "with secret pleasure" (*avec un secret plaisir*) to the sea's edge in order to gloat over the drama of a storm-tossed ship, whose passengers lift their hands toward heaven but nevertheless sink into the sea along with their wives, who are holding their children in their arms—that would seem to him an atrocity, if Lucretius were right. But Lucretius does not know what he is talking about. People hasten to witness such a drama out of curiosity, and curiosity is "a natural feeling in man" (*un sentiment naturel à l'homme*). Voltaire claims that not one of these sightseers would fail to undertake the most difficult measures to save the shipwrecked passengers if he could. In the same way, when someone is publicly hanged, curious people do not rush to their windows out of malevolence, as would be true if, on reflecting, they took pleasure in their own lack of involvement. Those are the alternatives: "not by comparison with oneself . . . but by curiosity alone" (*ce n'est pas par un retour sur soi-même . . . c'est uniquement par curiosité*).[50]

Voltaire also begins the article "Curiosity" in his *Dictionnaire philosophique* by quoting and translating the first verse of Book 2 of *De rerum natura*. Here he pretends to address the poet directly, interrupting him and telling him he is mistaken about ethics, just as he has always been mistaken about physics. It is only curiosity, Voltaire claims, that makes people stand on the beach and watch a ship in peril at sea.[51] Voltaire appeals to his own experience of such an enjoyment, which he says involved uneasiness and discomfort but had nothing to do with the sort of reflection that Lucretius imports into the spectator's situation. There was no secret comparison between his own security and the peril of others: "I was curious and sensitive" (*j'étais curieux et sensible*). This passion alone drives men to climb trees in order to observe the bloodbath of a battle or a public hanging. And it is not a human passion but one we share with apes and puppies.

Voltaire once saw himself in the figure of the shipwrecked man, when he escaped the Prussian king's snares in Frankfurt in 1753 and spent three weeks of his regained safety in Mainz, in order to dry "his clothes, soaked through during the shipwreck."[52] From Strasbourg, he wrote to the countess Lützelburg, on 22 August 1753, telling her that fate plays with poor mankind like a shuttlecock, even though the shortness of the day of life might lead us to expect an evening without storms: "It is terrible to end such a short and unhappy career in the midst of storms" (*Il est affreux de finir au milieu des tempêtes une si courte et si malheureuse carrière*). On 2 September, he wrote to the countess again, this time relativizing the possibility of a feeling of security to the ones saved from shipwreck as well as the spectator, by picturing the seafarers looking back, from the harbor, on their adventure; but he immediately destroys the security value of this image by voicing a hyperbolic doubt as to whether there is any safe haven in this world: "Sailors in port like to talk about their storms, but is there any port in this world? People shipwreck everywhere, even in a small brook" (*Les matelots aiment dans le port à parler de leurs tempêtes, mais y a-t-il un port dans ce monde? On fait partout naufrage dans un ruisseau*).

A year before the "shipwreck" during his escape from Berlin, in his philosophical tale *Micromégas*, Voltaire had introduced the larger-than-life spectator in the characters of the giant from Sirius and his companion from Saturn. The two space travelers arrive on earth, just as Maupertuis's famous expedition is sailing across the Baltic on its way back from Lapland. To mock his Berlin rival, Voltaire tells us that the newspapers had already reported the expedition's shipwreck. He attributes this event to the aliens' interest in what was for them a microscopically small vehicle and its passengers. What the human explorers had experienced as catastrophe was only the flip side of the theoretical interest the spectators from another planet had taken in them: the giant had very carefully laid the ship in the palm of his hand. His magnifying glass, which barely allowed him to perceive a whale and a ship, was not strong enough to reveal a being situated beneath the threshold of perceptibility: "a being as imperceptible as men are" (*un être aussi imperceptible que des hommes*). Human history is a cosmically unnoticeable event.

Voltaire expects the alien perspective of his cosmic giants to help his readers, too, to see human history as insignificant and to question the resources invested in it. Looking out his window at the Prussian king's tall grenadiers, he turns aside from his narrative to remark that their commander, had he an opportunity to read the book, would probably make their helmets even taller. This seems to him the most ludicrous way of compensating for man's post-Copernican insignificance. If we look back at Fontenelle's learned marquise, we note that here man has lost all opportunity of himself remaining a spectator in relation to his loftier cosmic companions: thinking himself a subject, he is in fact the pure object of alien measurement.

A decade later, in the article "Curiosity" in his philosophical dictionary, Voltaire goes still further to free the figure of the shipwreck spectator from the suspicion of reflective self-enjoyment, which Voltaire finds so dreadful. If one could imagine an angel flying down from the empyrean sphere in order to observe, through a crack in the earth, the sufferings of the damned in hell, and in this way to take pleasure in his own incapacity for suffering, then this angel would no longer be distinguishable from a devil. Even if he does not engage in this kind of secret reflection, the passion of curiosity would put man in unsavory company if it allowed him to take everything, even the experiments of physics, as merely a play produced for his amusement. Voltaire not only bases his judgment of the shipwreck spectator on his own experience ("Cela m'est arrivé") but also appeals to that experience in the passage in which he moves from the thought experiment with the angel to human nature: "On the basis of my own experience and that of all my fellow gawkers, I believe it is only curiosity that causes us to hurry to see any sight, of whatever kind" (*je pense par ma propre expérience et par celle de tous les badauds mes confrères, qu'on ne court à aucun spectacle, de quelque genre qu'il puisse être, que par curiosité*).[53] Man is a being so given to rubbernecking that, in his curiosity, he even forgets to be concerned about himself.

It is the Abbé Galiani who, in a letter to Madame d'Épinay written in Naples on 31 August 1771, flatly contradicts Voltaire's article and, in doing so, returns to the image of shipwreck and its spectator. He gives the image still another twist. Even if curiosity were the kind of passion Voltaire considers it to be, it would all the more require the assumption of an undisturbed standpoint that was protected from any risk. It is only because the spectator stands on firm ground that he is fascinated by the fateful drama on the high seas. Curiosity is a form of sensibility from which the slightest danger tears us away, forcing us to be concerned with ourselves alone.[54]

For this reason, the theater illustrates the human situation in its purest form, according to Galiani. Only when the spectators have been shown to their secure places can the drama of human imperilment be played out before them. This tension, this distance, can never be great enough: "The more safely the spectator sits there and the greater the danger he witnesses, the more intense his interest in the drama. This is the key to the secrets of tragic, comic, and epic art." Thus, Lucretius was not entirely wrong after all. Security and good fortune are conditions of curiosity, and the latter is a symptom of the former. A curious people is a great honor to its government, for the more fortunate a nation is, the more curious it will be. Hence Paris is "the capital of curiosity."

Finally, Galiani most violently contradicts Voltaire in disputing the claim that humans have curiosity in common with animals. Curiosity is a mark of man's ability to confront unfamiliar, exciting, extreme events without fear, whereas animals are terrified by such events. "One can frighten animals, but one can never make them curious." As the capacity for distance, curiosity is for Galiani an anthropological criterion. "Since animals are not capable of curiosity, the curious human is more human than any other. . . . As a curious being, man is receptive to every spectacle. Almost all sciences have arisen out of curiosity. And the key to everything lies in the security, in the unsuffering condition of the curious being."

Although in Galiani's whole letter there is no mention of seafaring and dry land, nevertheless the metaphorical background created by Lucretius is constantly present when security and danger, happiness and curiosity are seen as interdependent. The theatrical comparison, which is more powerful for Galiani, has moved into the foreground. It does not bother him that the spectator's "secure places" can no longer be described except in terms of the comfort of theater loges, into which no rain can fall. The need to attain an aesthetic level and to represent what is essentially human on that level admits the required distance between security and danger only as an artificial situation, and no longer a real one, as in the original metaphorical material. The danger is played on stage, and security is a rainproof roof. Through the move from seashore to theater, Lucretius's spectator is withdrawn from the moral dimension; he has become "aesthetic."

But the ascent to the aesthetic level is only one aspect of the repression of the shipwreck metaphor. The other is that the principle of inviolate nature and seafaring's crime against it have also dropped out. This is made very explicit in the eighth conversation in Galiani's *Dialogues sur le commerce des blés*. Man is a being of indeterminable greatness, Galiani says at the outset, and later on he adds that nature is also an immense and undefined something, with which man can neither ally himself nor skeptically come to terms. "With our little bit of art, our little bit of understanding, which God gave us, we take up the battle with Nature, and we often succeed in conquering and mastering her by turning her own powers against her."

Shipwreck is no longer the extreme image of the human situation in nature. The metaphor would no longer be suited to expressing what it once implied. It is the task of technology, of science, to deal with the problem of steering the ship. Since that is so, the shipwreck metaphorics can now stand for the prudence of public administration and its opposition to every sort of passion: "Enthusiasm and public administration are contradictory concepts, and even if we are entering the harbor of fragile evidence, we must never turn one side of the ship to the wind and the waves in such a way as to run it aground. That is the first rule: one lands, when one can, but one must land. . . . One must avoid great shocks, moderate one's movement, and seek the high sea, if one wants to avoid shipwreck."[55]

The earliest German reflection of the shipwreck-spectator configuration seems to be in an "Epigram" by Johann Joachim Ewald from the year 1755, titled "Der Sturm"[56]:

Suddenly it grows dark, the wind is howling loud,
And heaven, sky, and land appear a frightful jumble.

Toward the stars flies up the ship, then plunges down again,
Sails on washed by waves, with naught but ruin all around,
Here lightning, there thunder, the whole ether storming,
Swell towering up on swell, and cloud on cloud,
The ship is shattered, and I . . . nothing happened to me,
Because I only watched the storm from shore.

The undisturbed, aesthetic situation of the poetic "I" is presented to the reader as a punch line, modeled on awakening from a nightmare. This nonsimultaneity of experiencing and speaking privatizes the configuration. Only after the fact is one assured that the spectator position with regard to the most dreadful disaster has not been abandoned and can be maintained. The spectator's participation in the experience is assumed to be so intensive that it is as though he has to be reminded that he is not personally involved; to this extent, the reader's surprise is the artificial correlate of the author's pretended intensity of experience.

One should think again of Horace's ode (1.14), in which the ship, wretchedly battered by a storm at sea but not yet completely broken up, is chided by the spectator, who is full of foreboding and warns against further adventures on the way home to the harbor: "What are you doing? Sail for the port as fast as you can!" (*O quid agis? Fortiter occupa portum!*). There, however, the spectator is justified only because he can intervene, call for a return to land, as the one who perceives the condition of the ship more clearly from outside than those who are sailing it can.[57] In Horace, the spectator is affected in a different way: the one who sees more bears a heavier burden. Here, the "political" use of the image is already made available, even if it is not intended, and even if Quintilian's deciphering of the wretched boat as an allegory of the ship of state should not be considered unproblematic.[58]

To this extent, the poet may not have felt and meant what his commentator ascribes to him: that he had, in opposition to his Greek predecessor Alcaeus, "reduced the outbreak of terror among the wave-tossed sailors to the reflection of the sympathetic spectator, who observes from the shore the vessel battling against the elements."[59] As blind involvement, the poet's identification with the sailor and his predicament in Alcaeus's fragment was not automatically "stronger" than the warning given by the "seeing" spectator. Its intensity consists in the will to avert misfortune, which can only proceed, and penetrate, "from outside." On closer inspection, Alcaeus's sailor was "more" the spectator of his predicament than is the speaker in Horace. The former perceives the present state only as loss and the disordering of every kind of orientation, whereas the latter recognizes the present state of deceptive calm after the storm as unavoidable helplessness before every future test.

The question concerning the intensity of the poetic subject in each of the two cases is connected with the temporal relationship that the poem conjures up. One should not put Alcaeus in the preterit, because his "I" obviously has survived the storm (otherwise, he would not have been able to write a poem). This amounts to identifying the poet with his fictive "I." Such an approach must lead to a failure to notice the future-oriented use of the comparison in Horace, where what is acutely perceived only becomes the sign of an impending disaster that is unseen by the others.[60] The spectator's possession of options—however "politically" he may understand his perception of the impending calamity—was a presupposition, for Horace, of his being able to take over the Greek poet's image at all.

Even though there is no demonstrable connection between the two events, it is probably not wholly accidental that Ewald's poem "The Storm" was written in 1755, the year of the Lisbon earthquake, which was to put an end to metaphysical optimism of the kind represented by the German followers of Leibniz. In 1792, Herder called on the shipwreck-spectator metaphorics to depict the position of the German public with regard to the French Revolution. As early as 1769, when he set out by ship from Riga to France in order to study the Enlightenment at its source, he had been converted at sea: "and so I became a philosopher on board the ship—a philosopher, however, who had not yet learned how to philosophize from nature, without books or instruments."[61] The blank surface of the sea reminds him of the tabula rasa as the condition of the authenticity and autonomy of thought: "When will I have reached the point where I can destroy within myself everything I have learned from others, and begin discovering by myself what I think and learn and believe?" He still feels that he has not yet gotten beyond the antithesis between philosophizing from books and philosophizing from nature: "Had I known this, what a standpoint, sitting under a mast on the wide ocean, to philosophize about the sky, sun, stars, moon, air, wind, sea, rain, currents, fish, the sea floor, and to be able to discover the physics of all this by oneself! . . . The sea floor is a new earth! Who knows it? What Columbus and Galileo can discover it? What new deep-sea diving voyages and what new telescopes still remain to be discovered in this wide world?" However, Herder's encounter with leaders of the French Enlightenment associated with the *Encyclopédie* was evidently inadequate to the pathos of his great expectation. The voyage then produced a turning of the metaphor. On the return trip, in January 1770, Herder's ship went aground between Antwerp and Amsterdam. The sea as the site of self-discovery for the Sturm und Drang subject revealed itself as a foreign power.

As early as 1774, Herder described the current state of philosophy in terms of the shipwreck metaphor, not only as "doubt in a hundred forms" but also as "contradiction and sea surge: either we are wrecked, or what we are able to salvage in the way of morality and philosophy from the shipwreck is hardly worth talking about."[62] This is only one of the images that well up and are quickly overlaid in Herder's early sketch of his philosophy of history, which would be carried out a decade later in the first volume of his *Ideas on the Philosophy of the History of Mankind*.

Then in 1792, in the seventeenth of his *Letters for the Advancement of Humanity*, Herder takes stock of Germany's distance from the revolution among its neighbors.[63] This event has occupied and disturbed him more than he would have liked. He has often wished he "had not experienced these times." It is true that "the nature of this subject requires that one think about it and rationally reflect on its consequences"; distance is claimed, however, not only because of the separation between the event and the observer but still more because of the difference in national characters. This difference has already decided the distribution of roles between actors and spectators. Germany has in fact received from the papal court the honorable name of a "Land of Obedience," and any doubt concerning this characterization would be "a slander on the nation." The distance is determined above all by language, Herder writes, and this explains French drama's lack of success in Germany. On these assumptions, the spread of the revolutionary events to Germany seems out of the question.

When Herder resorts in this passage to the image of shipwreck and spectator, there remains a residue of uncertainty concerning the spectator's firm standpoint, which, in a surprising and paradoxical twist, is made subject to a demonologic condition: "We can observe the French Revolution as if it were a shipwreck on the open, foreign sea witnessed from the safety of the shore, as long as our evil genius does not throw us into the sea against our will."

It is worth noting that the connection between shipwreck metaphorics and theater metaphorics, established by Galiani, also appears in this text by Herder. The actual catastrophe is simultaneously a didactic drama "in God's book, the great world history," a drama—being played out before the eyes of a spectator already privileged by his national character— of a providence that "puts this scene itself before our eyes, for, after long preparations, it caused such things to occur in our times so that we might witness them and learn from them." The didactic situation is made possible only by the fact that these things occur outside one's own borders, and we ("on the condition, as I said, that an evil genius does not wantonly plunge us in") can take part in this event "only as we would in a newspaper story." Shipwreck and spectator are here only the superficial representation of the situation; at a deeper level, the shipwreck is a didactic drama staged by Providence. The spectator's security is threatened by the figure of the evil genius, who is capable of hurling him into the sea—the whole drama is set forth within the framework of this dualism of Providence and evil Genius. The metaphor is only a translation of a translation.

4. The Art of Survival

There is still, as Herder's strained exploitation of the metaphor shows, a spectator position with regard to history, even if it is no longer one of absolute inviolability. How difficult it had become to remain a spectator was shown at the beginning of the following century by Goethe's visit, in May 1807, to the site of the Battle of Jena. The conversation Goethe later had with the Jena historian Heinrich Luden (who would become the editor of the political and historical review *Nemesis*), which Luden reported in his memoir *Looking Back on My Life*,[64] has become famous. Sufficient reasons for this are that the German defeat at Jena in October 1806 had struck deeply into Goethe's life, and that this experience pointed forward to Goethe's meeting with Napoleon two years later, which also made a lasting impression on him. Luden's report shows that it was not Napoleon who first made Goethe into a disappointing partner for the German patriots in their defeat and their hopes of liberation; the spectator of the site of history at Jena was already not up to their expectations. This is expressed precisely in an allusion to Lucretius's comparison, and in this connection we must point out that the discussion took place at the home of Carl Ludwig von Knebel, whose translation of Lucretius would be published in 1821.[65]

Luden describes what he expected and what he saw. After the battle, he had inquired at every opportunity as to how Goethe had fared,[66] and he had in this way arrived at the belief that Goethe, "too, had had his cross to bear and had shared in the misery that a victorious enemy who is defiant and arrogant is accustomed to inflict on the vanquished and their defenseless dependents." And this is how he describes the man he met: "His face was very serious, and his behavior showed that the pressure of the time was on him, too. 'The man has felt it,' Knebel said." Luden gives an account of what he himself has experienced in Jena. Knebel then exclaims that it was horrible, it was monstrous. "Goethe, however, said a few words so softly that I did not understand them." The disappointment of the defeated patriot begins. He asks Goethe explicitly how it went with him, and Goethe replies with an allusion to the ancient spectator: "I have no grounds for complaint. Rather like a man who looks down from a solid cliff onto the raging sea and cannot help the shipwrecked men below but also cannot be reached by the breakers, and, according to some ancient, this is even supposed to be a comfortable feeling." At this point, the later translator of the work interrupts: "According to Lucretius!" and Goethe, confirming this and taking up the image again, continues: "Thus I stood there, safe and sound, and let the furious tumult pass by me."

Luden cannot deny that, on hearing these words spoken "with a certain comfortable air," he felt "a chill go through his heart." He tries to redeem them, suggesting that the misfortune of the individual evaporates when confronted by the monstrous misfortune of the fatherland, whose cause he could not give up for lost even in the time of humiliation and shame. Knebel agrees enthusiastically. "Goethe, however, did not say a word and showed nothing in his face."[67]

Nietzsche was to say of Goethe, "His life long he was a master of subtle silence."[68] But this silence after Jena, which is situated in terms of Lucretius's image, marks ironically the distance Goethe had traveled from his own youthful annoyance with spectatorship. On 25 August 1772, he had criticized Gessner's *Idylls* in the pages of the *Frankfurter Gelehrte Anzeigen*, the Sturm und Drang critical organ published by Merck. He had censured their lack of reality and humanity. The poem entitled "The Storm" he found "unbearable: Voltaire, from his bed in Lausanne, could not have observed the storm on Lake Geneva more calmly in his mirror than the people on the rock around whom the storm is raging describe to each other what they both see."[69] Once again, Voltaire is the spectator—represented as strange—of a storm. His mediated and sheltered relationship to reality becomes the devastating apostrophe of Goethe's critique of Gessner.

The mirror may in fact have been an intensifying addition by Goethe the reviewer. This question calls for a short excursus. In Voltaire's letters about the winter he spent in Lausanne, which Goethe may have known or which may underlie the anecdote, he speaks only of the view from his bed out over the lake. It has been suggested that Goethe's reference to Voltaire was based on Merck's experiences; in that case, however, Ferney must have been confused with Lausanne, because Merck had first visited Voltaire after 1760, at Ferney, in fact.[70] If this hypothesis were given weight, one would, however, have to set aside Voltaire's self-stylization in two letters, one written to de Moncrif on 27 March 1757 and the other to Thiriot on 2 June 1757, as possible bases for Goethe's suggestive image—exaggerated to the point of caricaturing the philosopher—of Voltaire looking out over the lake.[71] Both letters contain the most important requisite for idyllic distance, the bed: "From my bed I see the lake" (*Je vois de mon lit le lac*).

Voltaire himself had made his two houses in Geneva and Lausanne, both of which had views of the lake, into metaphors of his delightful distance from the kings of Europe whose favor he did not enjoy, and indeed of his situation as envied by them. In 1759, he wrote in his *Mémoires* that he possessed in these two domiciles what those princes could not give him, what in fact they would take away from him if they could: "peace and freedom" (*le repos et la liberté*)—and even occasionally what they could give but which he had not received from them, by which he means money, which he was fond of. He quotes his own programmatic epicurean poem of 1736 as now being fulfilled: "I am putting into practice what I said in *Le Mondain*" (*je mets en pratique ce que j'ai dit dans le Mondain*). At that time, he had concluded with a line intended to represent the connection he made between ethics and the capacity for happiness: "The earthly paradise is where I am" (*Le paradis terrestre est où je suis*). In the spectator's pose that Goethe apostrophizes, Voltaire had authorized himself, as an extraterritorial authority in unattainable autarky and with full self-empowerment, in opposition to the consequences of the Berlin adventure and the refusal to return to Paris.

All this is included in the offensiveness to Goethe of the "spectator," which is reflected in his review of Gessner's *Idylls*—this offensiveness being almost an anticipation of the disconcertedness with which Luden would take exception to Goethe's serenity after Jena. However, there is no indication that, by remembering his early derision of the spectator Voltaire, the visitor to the Jena battlefield could have better perceived or even comprehended his interlocutors' inability to understand his claim to the standpoint of the spectator on the rock.

Goethe stylized himself. His helplessness during the night of Weimar's occupation by Napoleon's troops—it was only through Christiane's stout-heartedness that he escaped the marauders—had bothered him. He did not yet know, on this May day in 1807, that he would have to defend his spectator's post against the conqueror's temptations, against Napoleon's eyes, during the meeting in Erfurt the next year.

Luden, too, will have stylized his recollection. It is aimed at the by-then-unchallengeable Goethe's hard-shelledness, which had been made a public issue by the Young Germany group. Everything is set up for the confrontation between the committed patriot and the Olympian spectator modeling himself on the ancients. As usual, the scenery of the epicurean didactic poem is translated into an illustration of historical positions and is focused on the offensive dubiousness of one of them.

What has changed? Lucretius had stressed humanity's liberation from fear. It was primarily events in nature—and only secondarily events in the human world, as a category of natural events—that could cause fear. Therefore, liberation was to be found, above all, in Epicurus's atomistic physics, which had taught that all possible explanations of natural events should be seen as equally valid and consequently a matter of indifference for men. Because they participate in this, human action and suffering, which are from birth to death processes of this same nature, must leave the man who understands these things unmoved. Shipwreck shows this: it is a natural event, and it is accidental that it involves people along with the ship. That man goes to sea at all and puts himself in such danger must, accordingly, also be a natural event, the result of his drives and passions—if the Roman Lucretius had not intended, by means of this philosophy, to denounce the hypercultivated degeneration of his world. Voltaire, by identifying curiosity as an animal drive, and thus as a natural event, had come closer to the heart of the philosophy than Lucretius had thought he could afford to come. The energy that drives us beyond the state of nature and the meager provision of the natural standpoint is itself a part of nature.

It is as if all this were forgotten on that day at Jena, for Goethe's inspection of the battlefield is free from all metaphorics. It makes up for, and takes the place of, the spectator's endurance in the face of the battle itself and its consequences. Above all, the spectator's self-discipline, which allows no outcry of distress and sympathy to be drawn from him, is distant from any naturalness of impulses. It is discipline in the classical—or what is taken to be classical—form: a high degree of artificiality. Not even philosophy—and this one least of all—is involved in the reserve, the holding back, the self-disengagement of this attitude.

At Jena, Goethe had not favored with a single word his enthusiastic conversation partner, who confessed that he would have been prepared to endure personal misfortune gladly if that had been able to turn the battle around. The observer of the battlefield appeals to the ancient poet's comparison precisely in order to protect *his* history from history per se,[72] insofar as the latter is always, and must remain, the history of others. However, it is no longer possible to put historical catastrophes on the same footing with physical ones. The point of physical catastrophes, in the philosophy of Epicurus and Lucretius, had been that they were fertile in forms, that they were the form-making power of nature itself. Goethe has no philosophy of history, and his aversion to Vulcanism, together with his affinity for Neptunism,[73] could suggest that he would have found atomism's catastrophic productivity illuminating neither in the case of nature nor in that of history. Before I pursue his assessment of Lucretius a step further, we must consider what, in fact, could have been done with the configuration of shipwreck and spectator, in the philosophy of history. To that end—how could it be otherwise?—we must glance at the philosopher of history par excellence. Only a sidelong glance, but with the question, could he make something of the Roman Epicurean's imagined scene in relation to his own concept of reason and reality?

Hegel alluded to Lucretius's metaphor in order to present freedom's self-production as a world, through history and the downfalls that are its means. Whereas in atomism the durability and regularity of natural forms had formed only the apparent foreground of the invisible, catastrophic play of the atoms, in Hegel, by contrast, the drama of passions and folly, of ills and evils, of the sinking of the most flourishing empires, which history places before our eyes, is only the means to the "true result of world history," that ultimate goal, for which "these monstrous sacrifices [have] been made."[74]

Here, too, the spectator's position is determined by reflection; it grants him more than consolation; it reconciles him with the "immediate prospect of history." And with unsurpassable intensity: it "transfigures reality with all its apparent injustices and reconciles it with the rational." What an achievement of reason it is when the spectator looks at the individuals in history, with "profound pity for [their] untold miseries," and sees their downfall as the work not only of nature but also of human will.

The spectator's sensitivity can be intensified to the "extreme pitch of hopeless sorrow with no redeeming circumstances" to provide the counterbalance that he is supposed to find, brought to the point where he sees "a most terrifying picture take shape," which finally—only as he returns from "the lassitude into which such sorrowful reflections can plunge us"—fades away in the demands of reality. The spectator can turn away from the "rebellion of the good spirit" within him, without thereby already being turned toward reason in the shape of the question about the meaning of the sacrifices. He can in fact also "retreat into that selfish complacency that stands on the calmer shore and, from a secure position, smugly look on at the distant spectacle of confusion and wreckage." To regard as only a means what is revealed when we "look on history as an altar on which the happiness of nations, the wisdom of states, and the virtue of individuals are slaughtered"—that is (however circuitously it may be expressed), at the end of all the wise sayings of the philosophy of history, the true security of the spectator in the position of reason. It is less a position than a "path of reflection," which makes it possible "to ascend from the spectacle of historical detail to the universal principle behind it."

To return to Goethe's allusion to the shipwreck-spectator configuration: in it we find no sympathy either with any reconciliation based on a philosophy of history or with Epicurus's philosophy. When Knebel's translation of Lucretius was finally published, it was Goethe who exerted himself to dissuade the translator from including a partisan preface and to urge him toward "simple points of view"—to make him "productive and positive."[75] In the claim of the philosophy that Lucretius celebrates, Goethe sees a violent overcoming of what he considers human. Lucretius's view of nature is "grandiose, ingenious, and lofty," but his thought about the ultimate grounds of things has the same character that he believed it would be liberating to make these grounds appear to have: it is "indifferent." One feels, Goethe says, that Lucretius's whole poem is inhabited by "a dark, wrathful spirit, who definitely wants to raise himself above the pitiful state of his contemporaries." We should note that when Goethe tries to characterize the philosophy of the didactic poem, it is once again nothing but a battle that comes to his mind. He suggests that the ancient poet can be compared with the Prussian king at the battle of Kolin, who, during an attack, had cried to his hesitating grenadiers, "Dogs! Do you want to live forever?" It is precisely the ambition to free humanity's relation to death, once and for all, from fear, that is made suspect by Goethe's comparison with the Prussian king's contempt for men.

Goethe's appeal to Lucretius's spectator thus has nothing to do with Lucretius's philosophy. His distance is not that of reflection but rather that of escape. When, on 21 October 1806, he informed Knebel of his marriage "with my little darling" and even dated the wedding ring to 14 October, the very day of the battle of Jena on which his existence had been threatened, he found this formula for the events and the destinies around Weimar and Jena: "What else can one expect in the moments of shipwreck!" If half a year later he could already compare himself with the spectator of a shipwreck, it was only because he knew that he and his world had barely escaped going under. From the battlefield at Jena, must he not have looked back with relief on the danger to which he had personally been exposed? If this looks different in Luden's account, if it looks like indifference with regard to the misfortune in battle of the multitudes and of the fatherland, one should not forget that another half-century of patriotic disappointments with Goethe's imperturbability concerning the general fate entered into this recollection.

The transformation of the spatial distance of the spectator of others' distress at sea into the temporal distance of looking back on one's own shipwreck also marks Goethe's use of the metaphor when, in 1812, he consoles his friend Zelter, whose son had committed suicide. One should feel pity rather than lay blame, he says, when weariness with life overcomes people. This is only another crossing over from another's fate to Goethe's own, whose mastering always immediately strikes him as typically human. Once, all the symptoms of that "strange disease, just as natural as it is unnatural," had also coursed through his inner being. *Werther*, he says, can leave no one in doubt about that. He knows only too well how many resolutions and strenuous efforts he had had to make "at that time, to escape the waves of death," just as he "also saved himself with difficulty and arduously recovered from many a later shipwreck." There follows a strange insertion in an expression of condolence: "But all sailors' and fishermen's stories are like that."

Here he has reverted entirely from consolation to the image of his own "story." Only in this connection, after all, can the genre of those "stories" be described as that of a retrospective and exalting living-through of danger: "After the nocturnal storm one gains the shore again, the drenched survivor dries off, and the next morning, when the brilliant sun again begins to shine on the sparkling waves, the sea already is hungry for figs again (*hat das Meer schon wieder Appetit zu Feigen*)." Where does this extraordinary conclusion come from?

In 1781, Goethe had already used it in the poem that begins "In the sunset the sea and sky lie calm" (*Im Abendrot liegt See und Himmel still*), in order to represent once again the old estrangement, introduced by Hesiod, between a man who cannot resist the seductions of the sea and another who quietly returns to his land and does not reject the little cares of a limited existence. The enigmatic expression "back into the sea, which wants figs again" (*Zurück ins Meer, das wieder*

Feigen will) stands for precisely this temptation to set out abroad. The one who stays wishes the traveler luck but has little confidence that such wishes for the daring sea voyage will be fulfilled: "You were warned; you seemed secure, / now may both profit and loss be yours" (*Du warst gewarnt; du schienst geborgen, / Nun sei Gewinst und auch Verlust sei dein*).

Three decades later, almost forgetting his duty to console his friend Zelter, Goethe applied this topos to his own experience. He was fond of collections of sayings, and he was practiced and liberal in forming and transforming sayings. He could have taken this one from the *Adagia* of Erasmus of Rotterdam, who for his part ascribes it to virtually all the collections of sayings from antiquity that were available to him. In the form entitled *Siculus mare*, it is the punch line of the story of a man from Sicily who had undergone shipwreck while carrying a cargo of figs, and another time sits on the beach and sees before him the sea lying gentle and calm, as if wanting to entice him to undertake another voyage. Thereupon he expresses his unseduceability in these words: "Oid' ho theleis, syka theleis"—"I know what you want: you want figs!" As Erasmus interprets it, this is supposed to apply to everyone who is tempted to expose himself to danger a second time and against his own experience.[76]

But it was only years after his first use of the topos in a lyric that Goethe had the bodily experience whose metaphorical use seems to come so naturally to him. This is truly what he was to call a sailor's or fisherman's tale, a secret identification with Odysseus in the Sirens episode. On the voyage back from Messina to Naples, in May 1787, he found himself not in a violent storm, as some think, but in a lull in the winds that prevented the vessel from navigating. To crash on the Siren cliffs beyond Capri would not have been a despicable fate. But they only "nearly went down, in the strangest way, with a completely clear sky and completely calm seas, as a result of this very becalming."[77] This, too, went directly into the poem. For the sailor the worrisome "deathly calm" (*Todesstille*) of a peaceful sea without movement is "dreadful" (*fürchterlich*)! The poem entitled "Glückliche Fahrt" ("Fortunate Voyage") is the counterpart of "Meeres Stille" ("Calm on the Seas"): the return of the winds, Aeolus himself stirring up the fixity, releases the "fearful bond."

Toward the end of the fifteenth book of *Dichtung und Wahrheit*, Goethe goes beyond the metaphorics of shipwreck, and even beyond that of the distance of life from the experience of failure. What happens on the sea, he says, is as if it did not happen. For this, he finds the metaphor of ships' courses across the sea that disappear without a trace. By means of this metaphor, he indicates the vain historical pride taken by the outgoing century of the Enlightenment in the belief that its accomplishments could not be lost, that its paths, having been found, would be continued. The crisis of this self-consciousness had become clear to Goethe in the dispute about his "Prometheus," which had involved Jacobi, Lessing, and Mendelssohn, and which he describes in the same book of his memoirs. It was an epoch of high expectations, he says, since it insisted on attaining something that no one had yet attained and regarded it, on the basis of what had already been achieved, as attainable. "It was maintained that the path had been opened, forgetting that in earthly things a path can very rarely be spoken of: for, as the water that is dislodged by a ship instantly flows in again behind it, so also error, by the law of its nature, when eminent minds have once driven it aside and made room for themselves, very quickly closes up again behind them."[78]

This was written in 1814. Hence the expression of excessive demands could be immediately followed by an expression of resignation. The briefest formula for this experience that "the absurd in fact fills up the world." The murderous moralistic impatience of the court physician Zimmerman, whose contentious figure introduces the excursus on the outcome of the period, was unwilling to recognize this. One can discern the function of the metaphor of the trackless sea in the fact that the word "naturgemäss" [by the law of its nature] is emphatically added to it. For Goethe, it is always the relationship between history and nature that is at stake. It is only the most general expression for the conditions of this difference that vessels passing through the sea leave no trace on it; thus total events there cannot be surveyed and grasped and, for that very reason, cannot be translated into the reliability of irreversibility. Both progress and sinkings leave behind them the same peaceful surface.

5. The Spectator Loses His Position

Only a few years after Goethe's reference to Lucretius, and in the immediate temporal vicinity of his metaphor of tracklessness, Schopenhauer calls on the shipwreck-spectator configuration. He fully decodes the identicalness of the human subject in both positions, the position of those who are going down and that of the spectator. To this end, he makes use of the framework of his system, with its distinctive concept of reason as the representation of a representation and hence the instrument of distancing from the immediacy of life. It is reason that can make man into the spectator of what he himself suffers. As he succeeds in achieving pure observation of his constant entanglement with reality, he achieves a "comprehensive view of life as a whole." This already allows Schopenhauer to bring in the nautical metaphorics. This is because in its overview of life, the rational being's relation to the animal "is like that between a ship captain, who by means of his chart, compass, and quadrant knows accurately his course and his position at any time upon the sea, and uneducated sailors who see only the waves and the heavens."[79] Man leads two lives, one concrete and one abstract. In the first, he is "prey to all the storms of actual life, and to the influence of the present, and must struggle, suffer, and die like the brute." In the second, he stands next to, if not over, himself, with the miniaturized outline of his life's path before him. From this distance, "what strongly moves and completely possesses him in the first case, appears to him cold, colorless, and for the moment external to him; here he is merely the spectator, the observer."

This double life of the subject, which is closer to Hegel's contrivances than its admirers might like to admit, finds its purest expression in the feeling of the sublime. In the face of the most powerful natural events, this feeling combines the consciousness of self-endangerment and self-elevation, as it frees itself from identity with the will to live and attains the peace of contemplation, in spite of the difficulties of naked existence. Sublimity consists in elevation above the interest of the will, which, in "the large scale battle of the raging elements," makes itself its goal. When we are "abroad in the storm of tempestuous seas," then, "in the undismayed beholder, the two-fold nature of his consciousness reaches the highest degree of distinctness. He perceives himself, on the one hand, as an individual, as the frail phenomenon of will, which the slightest touch of these forces can utterly destroy, helpless against powerful nature, dependent, the victim of chance, a vanishing nothing in the presence of stupendous might; and, on the other hand, as the eternal, peaceful, knowing subject, the condition of the object, and, therefore, the supporter of this whole world; the terrific strife of nature only his idea; the subject itself free and apart from all desires and necessities, in the quiet comprehension of the Ideas."[80] In reflection, the spectator surpasses himself, becoming the transcendental spectator.

This transcendental spectator's distance from the enormities of nature is not only that of the rocky shore but also that of self-consciousness, for which all this has become his representation. If the heavens at night "force on our consciousness the immensity of the universe," there rises up "against such lying impossibility" something like transcendental defiance; the multiplicity of worlds exists "only" in and through our representation: "The vastness of the world, which disquieted us before, rests now in us; our dependence on it is annulled by its dependence on us."

Even if, in the "feeling" of sublimity, this does not yet achieve the full turning of reflection but is rather a borderline case of immediate and felt consciousness, it is nonetheless at the same time the protruding tip of reflection. Seizing it awakens the subject to the whole philosophy of its double role. It can come to grief, in this metaphorics, if it falls back out of the spectator position and becomes entangled with the world through the will, which exposes it to nature's menaces instead of setting it over against nature.

Schopenhauer understood Lucretius's configuration, where he cites it, above all as the distance of remembering, and that distance once again as the subject's shift to the standpoint of contemplation—as if he had had to understand Goethe on the Jena battlefield and to correct the witness's disconcerted misunderstanding. All that is given us directly is pain; "satisfaction and pleasure we can only know indirectly through the remembrance of the preceding suffering and want."[81] Remembering a peril that one has survived is precisely "the only means of enjoying the present blessings." It is only a sort of aid to such remembrance, its surrogate, when the sight or description of the sufferings of others "affords us satisfaction or pleasure in precisely the way Lucretius beautifully and frankly expresses it." Schopenhauer quotes the Proem in detail; its thesis, he says, is absorbed into the proposition that all happiness is "essentially only *negative* and never positive."

From the immediate preparations for, or at least the temporal vicinity of, his major work come two posthumously published notes that indicate even more productively his connection to the imaginative background of Lucretius's configuration. The first dates from 1816 and raises the question of why, in representing life, epic or dramatic poetry can never describe complete or enduring happiness but only happiness that is coming into being or sought after. One might expect and accept that the answer will serve and comply with the metaphysics of the will, of which life has become the phenomenal expression. The will—and this is already its classical determination—goes into the infinite and can end only by transcending itself; this occurs, as great passion or as pure cognition, in the genius. Schopenhauer's formula of the "life of the genius" is a paradox, for genius is distinguished precisely by not belonging to life, since it is completely filled with pure cognition as distance from life. Therein consists once again the happiness of theory: the Epicurean spectator of shipwreck is brought close to the ancient ideal of leisure and contemplation, because his distance now is only distance from life as the tumult and pressure of the human world. In the end, Schopenhauer brings to the surface the way he gets his orientation from the Roman's didactic poem, but since he sees the violence of the sea and the distress of the ship not as a metaphor for the "nature of things," as seen by atomism, but entirely for the real pain of the will that is dominant in man, he must also characterize the egoism of contemplation as morally dubious: "Just as we learn to love our present condition only through remembering earlier peril, so the sight of another person has the same effect; hence Lucretius: *suave mari magno caet*—and this is also the source of all genuine wickedness."[82]

It is true that what the spectator sees is his past, insofar as he has been able to become a spectator at all, to learn to love the "wisdom" of a standpoint withdrawn from life. But what he sees also lies before him in the future, as that which inevitably proceeds from life, which is "a sea full of rocky cliffs and whirlpools." He avoids these with care and caution, although he knows that the success of "all the effort and skill expended in making his way through" only brings him nearer the point at which his crack-up becomes inevitable. He knows that in this very way he "comes with every step forward closer to, indeed he even steers toward, the greatest, the total, inevitable, and incurable shipwreck: death." The latter is not only the ultimate goal of one's efforts but "worse than all the rocky cliffs that one evaded."[83]

For the functioning of the metaphorics of existence, there is a close affinity between the basic themes of seafaring and theater.[84] In Galiani's reaction to Voltaire's ethical integration of curiosity, the spectator metaphor had already unexpectedly turned into the theatrical scenario. In Schopenhauer as well, his often-preferred image, which is drawn from the theatrical sphere, overlaps the nautical image. This is entirely plausible if the interiorized double role of the single subject—on the one hand, tossed about by storms and threatened by death, on the other, reflecting on his situation—is to be presented. In his withdrawal into reflection, man resembles "an actor who has played his part in one scene, and who takes his place among the audience until it is time for him to go on the stage again, and quietly looks on at whatever may happen, even though it be the preparation for his own death (in the piece), but afterward again goes on the stage and acts and suffers as he must."[85] Whatever serenity is possible for human beings proceeds from this doubleness of life. It is expressed in the fact that "in accordance with previous reflection, or a formed determination, or a recognized necessity, a man suffers or accomplishes in cold blood what is of the utmost and often terrible importance to him." There at last, one might truly say, "reason manifests itself practically." The fullest development of practical reason is represented, Schopenhauer says, in the ideal of the Stoic sage.

Who continues the play when the actor definitively withdraws, to become a spectator? The simile permits only one answer: the play then ceases to be performed at all; the tragedy does not take place.

This is the other answer to the simple question asked by the Enlightenment as to whether the calm sea of fully achieved insight could really be the solution to the problem of reason. The answer already mentioned was that being becalmed is lethal to life; the sail must be filled by the driving winds of the passions. This was also directed against neo-

Stoicism and its ideal of *ataraxia*, the classical domestication of the *passiones*, which was important for the foundation of modernity. When he seeks to represent both the life drive and the transition to contemplation by means of a *single* image, Schopenhauer makes the sailor in the midst of storms a stoic. Nothing need be said about the ship's voyage and goal, because it has become wholly the vehicle of surviving [*Überleben*] and rising above life [*Über-Leben*]. "Just as a sailor sits in a boat trusting to his frail barque in a stormy sea that is unbounded in every direction, rising and falling with the howling mountainous waves, so, in the midst of a world of sorrows, the individual man sits quietly, supported by, and trusting to, the *principium individuationis*, or the way in which the individual knows things as appearances."[86] In spite of the stormy conditions invoked here, that amounts almost to the tranquillity of Dionysus's sea voyage as depicted on Exekias's ancient vase. Just as Lucretius's spectator no longer needs a sailor in peril at sea, because he projects his own past or future distress into the image of the raging sea, so the sailor in his little boat no longer needs a spectator on the shore, because he himself has become, or is about to become, a world spectator.

The reader of Heine's pamphlet on Ludwig Börne, which he himself ambiguously termed a "Denkschrift,"[87] will never forget the cynicism of the scene in which the author imagines his meeting on the high seas with his shipwrecked counterpart, on whom he casts a spectator's glance, only to sail past him. What merits our attention here is not the metaphorical scene itself but rather the grounds on which the contemporary, the eyewitness, turns away.

First of all, there is a reversal of the situation. Heine describes the three days he spent in Börne's company in

Frankfurt, in 1815, which "flowed by in almost idyllic peacefulness." At the time of writing, he is looking back at this across a quarter-century. As he departed in the mail coach, Börne had looked after him for a long time, "as melancholy as an old sailor who has retired to dry land, and who feels moved to sympathy when he sees a young jackanapes who is going to sea for the first time. . . . The old man thought at that time that he had said farewell forever to the malicious element and that he would be able to spend the rest of his days in the safe harbor!"[88]

The expectation was not to be fulfilled, and this leads to the reversal of the situation. "Soon afterward, he had to return to the high seas, and there our ships passed by each other, during the raging of the dreadful storm, in which he went down." Heine is referring to Börne's becoming a republican and his participation in the aftermath of the July revolution of 1830, during which he moved away from Heine, considering him the representative of a politically unreliable aestheticism. But what Heine published concerning Börne in 1840 already concerned a dead man, whose image in the political shipwreck he conjured up: "He was standing at the wheel of his ship, defying the impetuousness of the waves. . . . Poor man! His ship had no anchor and his heart had no hope. . . . I saw how the mast broke, how the wind tore away the rigging. . . . I saw how he stretched out his hand toward me." Heine confesses that he did not grasp the outstretched hand. He asserts, moreover, that he was right not to have done so, for he thus avoided endangering the precious cargo, the sacred treasures that had been entrusted to him. This is the frightful formula of all those who refuse the little humanity of the present in order to fulfill the allegedly greater humanity of the future. So the expression used by the poet who sails past the shipwrecked man is of the most singular and frigid precision: "I was carrying on board my ship the gods of the future."

The point toward which the reception history of the shipwreck-spectator configuration tends is the dissolution of its original relationship to nature. Considered quantitatively, the nineteenth century was surely *the* epoch of shipwrecks. Down to the sinking of the *Titanic*, nature's force manifested itself more convincingly than ever before; in the nineteenth century, England alone lost five thousand men a year through ships going down—off the British coast there were 700 shipwrecks in the first six months of 1880, and in the first six months of 1881, 919[89]—in whose memory J. M. W. Turner set up a last fierce monument of romantic longing for death. In spite of this reality, the shipwreck metaphorics was completely occupied by the newly emerging historical consciousness and its insoluble dilemma of theoretical distance versus living engagement.

In the conclusion to the chapter "On Good and Bad Fortune in World History"—a lecture given in 1871—in the *World-historical Observations* that he prepared for the press (though he did not give them this title), Jacob Burckhardt introduced the Lucretian motif. It completes his idea of the integration of human history, whose unity "appears to us, at the end, like the life of *one* man." Although Burckhardt had earlier rejected as mere wishful thinking the trust in a secret balance between downfall and ascent, loss and gain, in the total life of humanity, still he clings to a continuity that persists through downfalls and new beginnings, as an "essential interest of our human existence."

The examination and pursuit of this unity then make claims on the historian in such a way that "the concepts of fortune and misfortune in comparison increasingly lose their meaning." This way of privileging knowledge over fortune looks like cold objectivity, but it is only resignation with regard to the fact that the wishes of individuals and peoples are blind and cannot serve to guide the observer. Thus, the historian's refusal to decide between fortune and misfortune is an acknowledgment of the subjectivity of these concepts that guards against arbitrariness, but it is not "indifference toward a wretchedness that may indeed involve us as well—through which we are protected against any coldly objective dealings." Nevertheless, Burckhardt regards the present from which he speaks as so rich in great decisions to be made (between deceptive peace and the approach of new wars; between the political forms of the leading civilized peoples and the increasing consciousness of suffering and impatience that result from broader education and communication) that the historian cannot resist "thinking of it as a marvelous drama"—even if not "for contemporaries, earthly beings"—and cannot resist pursuing the subject of this history, the "spirit of humanity," which seems to be building itself "a new dwelling place." This is all expressed in the subjunctive of irreality; what allows this spectator to be thought of is at the same time what prevents him from being realized in the historian: "A man who had a sense of this would completely forget fortune and misfortune and live on in pure longing for this knowledge." That is the last sentence in this reflection, pursued in so complicated a modality—complicated because it wants at all costs to avoid looking like a passage from Hegel.

Before that, however, the image from Lucretius had been conjured up for this imagined spectator—the unreal embodiment of the historian's good fortune without respect to good or bad fortune in history itself—and immediately let go again as an unattainable exteriority: "If we could wholly renounce our individuality and observe the history of the coming time with just as much tranquillity and concern as we do the drama of nature—for instance, as we might look at a storm at sea from dry land—then perhaps we would consciously witness one of the greatest chapters in the history of the spirit."[90] It is important that the fiction is related to the history that is impending, the epoch of the coming decisions.

On three occasions, each two years apart, Burckhardt applied the metaphorics of shipwreck to the past—though in his judgment not yet concluded—period of revolutions.[91] The first version of his *Einleitung in die Geschichte des Revolutionszeitalters* is dated 6 November 1867.[92] Burckhardt sees a consciousness of provisionality as the result of this period and also as the dominant feeling of his own present time. The outlook is gloomy: "Times of dread and deepest woe may be coming." There follows immediately the radical and, if we did not know better, last possible transformation of the seafaring metaphor, along with its full denaturalization through the elimination of the dualism of man and reality: "We would like to know the waves on which we sail across the ocean; but we ourselves are these waves."

The metaphor that has been pushed to the point of paradox is supposed to illustrate the epistemological position of the historian of the revolutionary period. This first becomes fully clear in the 1869 version. The historian is confronted by an unprecedented problem of objectivity, which, however, is something that historical knowledge is not allowed to abandon. "As soon as we rub our eyes, we clearly see that we are on a more or less fragile ship, borne along on one of the million waves that were put in motion by the revolution. We are ourselves these waves. Objective knowledge is not made easy for us."

There is no longer a firm standpoint from which the historian could be a distanced spectator. He can gain no view of the whole of the epoch, which is "perhaps only, relatively speaking, in its beginnings." But he can say what characterizes it: "the spirit of eternal revision." People have again and again thought they had reached the conclusion of the changes. Now we know "that one and the same storm, which swept over humanity in 1789, also carries us farther on." It is no longer the winds of the passions that keep humanity's affairs in motion and only occasionally get out of control in bad weather; it is the same storm that destroys and moves, causes break-ups and drives us further—a process that "stands in opposition to all the known past of our globe." The historian, who is carried along by this movement as well, must not, however, abandon himself to its motive forces—not to its wishes, and certainly not to its great, optimistic will. The task of knowing requires that he make himself "as free as possible from foolish joy and fear."

In connection with this apparently Epicurean postulate stands the third version of the metaphorical paradox, written down on 6 November 1871: "As soon as we become conscious of our situation, we find ourselves on a more or less fragile ship, which is carried along on one of the million waves. But one could also say: We ourselves are this wave, in part." The "in part" mitigates the sharpness of the paradox: the historian's chances no longer seem so wholly hopeless in this third attempt. But this passage is immediately preceded by an apostrophe that pushes pessimism all the way to eschatology: "(How long our planet will continue to tolerate organic life and how soon, with its paralysis, with the exhaustion of carbonic acid and water, earthly humanity will disappear is a question we need not take up.)"

With this dating, we have caught up with the sixth of the *World-historical Observations*, whose lecture plan is dated 7 November 1871, the day after the third version of the shipwreck metaphor.

Burckhardt had already boasted early on about his personal experience of what he was to come to understand about the phenomena of the revolutionary period. At age twenty-six he writes, "I consider it one of the most fortunate coincidences of my life that I came to know and understand at first hand the radicalism of all the important nations—that I perceived and could study in living examples, though in part against my will, the political mechanisms of the Carbonaro as well as the Paris radical, of the 'Free' Berliner as well as the shouter at the Basel festival."[93]

A quarter-century later, this experience makes its imprint above all in the *Observations'* chapter on historical crises; and it does so, not accidentally, in a version of the ship metaphor—tending toward paradox—which circles around the elementary fact registered by a phenomenology of historical crises, that in these situations those who are being driven take themselves to be the drivers: "The many-colored and strongly windblown sail considers itself the cause of the ship's movement, while it only catches the wind, which can shift and stop at any moment."[94]

The impossibility of the spectator, and the near impossibility of the historian, is the concluding point of Burckhardt's paradoxical sharpening of the metaphorical theme. Over against the uniqueness of an object into which it sees itself as integrated, theory discovers something that one might later have called its "existential" involvement. In the passages Burckhardt eliminated from his text on the introduction to the history of the revolutionary period, it also becomes clear, at least, how almost indissolubly the statement's intention is bound to the metaphor complex. In the third version, of 1871, he has still struck out a passage that reads like an interpretation of the first version of the metaphor. Loudly and from all sides, he says, a history of the revolutionary period is demanded, and the subject is "interesting in the highest degree; that is, it awakens the interests." The transition from "interesting" to "interests," to this already suspicion-arousing plural, makes it natural to raise the question of the "purity" of the theoretical object. Burckhardt formulates it as the question "whether this is an academic subject." If one takes the claim to knowledge in an absolute sense, knowledge proceeds only "from areas that are kept pure, closed off, withdrawn from purposes and passions." The present stands far too close to the time that is to be studied, which is still that of people's fathers and grandfathers. That time is "of a piece with the history of our own time, and its destructive and constructive forces continue to operate today." The result, however, is that considering it leads unavoidably "from the realm of the intellect to that of the will." The latter is described as a great optimistic will, which aims at what is never to be fulfilled. It deals with reality "as if the world were a tabula rasa," starting out from the conviction that "everything can be realized through correctly devised arrangements." From this basic premise the great conflicts arise, the outer ones from the inner ones. The interpretation of this result—skepticism regarding the historian's overview—makes Burckhardt resort once again to the nautical metaphorics: "Every later opinion regarding the 'how?' would be deceptive, even though, in and of itself, it would be a pardonable curiosity to ask on which wave of this sea we are presently being borne along."[95]

6. Shipbuilding out of the Shipwreck

Can it be that only the historian, anticipating the concept of "historicity," sees the interrelation of the subject and history as indissoluble, as Burckhardt, with his paradoxical metaphorics, sought to represent it and at the same time to express it in its unrepresentability? Naturally, the narrower range of sources in the natural sciences makes it especially difficult to answer this question, to surpass this supposed limitation. But the self-consciousness of the exact sciences in the nineteenth century also has its rhetoric. Among its highlights and most enduring effects is what was said by the main speaker at the Berlin Academy of Sciences, Emil Du Bois-Reymond, a founder of physiology, on academic occasions and in connection with jubilees.

In his lecture on Leibniz Day, 1876, speaking of Darwin's theory of natural selection, Du Bois-Reymond said: "We may henceforth, while we hold fast to this doctrine, feel like a man who would otherwise helplessly sink, were it not that he clings to a plank that barely holds him above the water. In a choice between the plank and going under, the advantage is decidedly on the side of the plank."[96] The imaginative character of this (if anything) positivistic self-understanding of science can be described as a "nautical accommodation" or, in a more recent mode, "living with shipwreck." One has to be prepared to be borne along on the sea indefinitely; no one talks any more about voyages and courses, landings and harbors. Shipwreck has lost its story setting. What has to be said is that science does not achieve

---

what our wishes and claims had expected of it, but what it does achieve is essentially unsurpassable and suffices to meet the demands of maintaining life.

In 1880, again on the academy's Leibniz Day, Du Bois-Reymond, in what is probably his most famous address, "The Seven Riddles of the World," comes back to his shipwreck simile. The fourth of his riddles gives him the occasion to point out that the difficulty of explaining the "apparently purposeful, teleological arrangement of nature" is indeed great, but not "absolutely transcendent." In the theory of natural selection, Du Bois-Reymond argues, Darwin had offered the possibility of at least getting around the assumption of an inner teleology of organic creation. At this point, the speaker quotes his own earlier lecture verbatim and comments, in opposition to the unwelcome applause of those who thought they were being presented with an image of the failure of reason, that his concern had been with the degree of probability of that explanation. "The fact that I compared the theory of selection to a plank on which a shipwrecked man sought rescue aroused such satisfaction on the other side that, in retelling the story, people enjoyed turning the plank into a straw."[97] The "other side" does not consist, in the speaker's sarcastic address, of the opposition alone.[98]

The plank is the most that can be expected in the human situation of immanent self-help through science, and the belittling straw converts into an image higher requirements than theoretical ones. Du Bois-Reymond insists, therefore, on the important difference between his plank and the straw that has been foisted on him: "The man who relies on a straw will sink, whereas a solid plank has saved many a human life." In any case—so it should surely continue—as long as one cannot expect a rescuing ship, "the fourth difficulty is, for the present, not transcendent, however hesitantly a serious and conscientious thinker may again and again stand before it." Can we ever move beyond the plank? Nothing needs to be said about that, even in a celebratory speech. The economy is one of self-preservation, not one of navigation toward landings and harbors, and certainly not one that takes into account firmly situated spectators.

In the reception histories of metaphors, the more sharply defined and differentiated the imaginative stock becomes, the sooner the point is reached where there seems to be an extreme inducement to veer around, with the existing model, in the most decisive way and to try out the unsurpassable procedure of reversing it.

The shipwreck metaphorics appears to have escaped such a reversal, even if the image process does seems to be wound backward by considering the shipwrecked man and his efforts to salvage, from what was almost the end of his sea voyage, a Robinson Crusoe–like new beginning of self-preservation. A reversal in the strict sense would be present only if the helpless man borne along on his plank at sea were the initial situation, that is, if the construction of a ship were only the result of self-assertion proceeding from this situation. In the "existential" use of the image type, which takes the always-already of embarkation and later the always-already of shipwreck as its point of departure, this is out of the question.

Nevertheless, turning the "nautical accommodation" toward a seaworthiness situated in the opposite temporal direction is almost a natural metaphor in a constructivist environment. In 1965, Paul Lorenzen contrasted the position of logical positivism to his own by means of an antithesis between two versions of the basic nautical metaphor.[99] He argued that the question concerning the methodical beginning of human thinking has been taken out of the realm of the rational, on the one hand by the predominance of axiomatic method after the displacment of Kant, and on the other by a hermeneutics oriented toward language philosophy. From the proposition that knowledge cannot go back behind life, the new immediacy of philosophy proceeding from Wilhelm Dilthey unintentionally produced the other proposition, that the expression "life," too, refers only to a contingent set of presuppositions, which manifests itself as a linguistic framework imposed on thought. Logical positivism, Lorenzen goes on, then narrows the formulation of the question to how the foundation of scientific language is possible. The answer to this question is supposed "to be given most clearly in an image, according to which language with its syntactic rules is a ship in which we find ourselves— on the condition that we can never enter a harbor. All repairs to or rebuilding of the ship must be carried out on the high seas." This is the "nautical accommodation" on a higher comfort level than the plank could offer. But apparently with such defects in the vehicle system that rebuilding and repairs have to be undertaken while under way. Nevertheless, the syntactical scaffolding functions so long as it can be kept afloat, and one need not, or cannot, inquire into the memory of where and when it was put into service.

Lorenzen is clearly referring to Otto Neurath's version of the ship simile, which Neurath directed against Rudolf Carnap's "fiction of an ideal language constructed out of tidy atomic sentences."[100] According to Neurath, there is no way to put a language of definitively certain protocol sentences at the beginning of scientific knowledge. Even if all metaphysics can be eliminated without remainder, the presuppositionlessness of such an absolute beginning cannot be achieved. The two reductions, that of metaphysics and that of the inexactitude of language, are separable. Neurath expresses this state of affairs by means of the ship metaphor: "We are like sailors who have to rebuild their ship on the high seas, without ever being able to take it apart in a dock and reconstruct it out of the best parts. Only metaphysics can disappear completely. The imprecise 'clusters' [*Ballungen*] are always somehow part of the ship." If imprecision is diminished in one place, it may reappear in a stronger form elsewhere.

That is the position that Lorenzen sets himself off against, with his extreme variant of the metaphor. The acknowledgment that we can neither spontaneously put the vehicle of natural language into use nor abandon it, because it is already decisively pregiven in everything else we can do—this concession in no way decides in advance the question of whether we ourselves must use this same apparatus in order to make possible the methodical fulfillment of the postulated beginning. Lorenzen continues the image by representing natural language as "a ship at sea," without thereby wanting to put the situation beyond any genetic inquiry into whence and whither. How this imbrication of pregivenness and presuppositionlessness is to be understood is illustrated by the reversal of the shipwreck metaphor: "If there is no attainable solid ground, then the ship must already have been built on the high seas; not by us, but by our ancestors. Our ancestors, then, were able to swim, and no doubt—using scraps of wood floating around—they somehow initially put together a raft, and then continually improved it, until today it has become such a comfortable ship that we do not have the courage any more to jump into the water and start all over again from the beginning."

The weakness of the metaphor when built up into a full comparison is clearly that it encourages arguments against leaving the comfortable ship. It makes the risk involved in jumping in and starting over from the swimming *status naturalis* seem hardly defensible. Even if one considers the philosophical zero point possible and unavoidable as the ultimate challenge in historical situations, and can even feel the fascination of critical destruction down to the point of an "as if" of history that never happened, one still cannot escape from the rhetoric that resides—against the intention of the user who is prepared to wager, to take a risk—within the turning of the metaphor. It strengthens the inclination, on that comfortable ship, to once again become the spectator of those who possess and want to spread the courage to leap into the water and start all over from the beginning, possibly counting on returning to the undamaged ship as the last preserve of a despised history.

Thus to think the beginning means, in the context of the comparison, to imagine the situation without the mother ship of natural language and, apart from its buoyancy, to "reperform," in a thought experiment, "the actions by means of which we—swimming in the middle of the sea of life—could build ourselves a raft or even a ship." The demiurgical, Robinson Crusoe longing of the modern age is also present in the handiwork of the constructivist who leaves home and heritage behind in order to found his life on the naked nothingness of the leap overboard. His artificially produced distress at sea does not come about through the frailty of the ship, which is already an end result of a lengthy process of building and rebuilding. But the sea evidently contains material other than what has already been used. Where can it come from, in order to give courage to the ones who are beginning anew? Perhaps from earlier shipwrecks?

Prospect for a Theory of Nonconceptuality

A metaphoris autem
abstinendum philosopho.
—Berkeley, *De motu* 3

When Erich Rothacker included my essay "Paradigms for a Metaphorology" in his *Archiv für Begriffsgeschichte*,[1] we were both thinking about a subsidiary method for the history of concepts that was just then emerging. In the interim, metaphorology's function has not changed, but its referent has, primarily in that metaphorics is now understood as merely a limited special case of nonconceptuality.

Metaphorics is no longer regarded primarily as the leading sphere for experimental theoretical conceptions, as the front line of concept formation, as a makeshift in situations in which technical terminology has not yet been consolidated, but is seen rather as an authentic way of grasping connections, one that cannot be limited to the narrow nucleus of "absolute metaphor."[2] The latter, too, was after all at first defined only by the fact that it could not be "replaced by literal predicates" on the same level of speech. One might say that the perspective has been reversed: it is no longer directed mainly toward the constitution of conceptuality but back toward the connections with the life-world as the constant motivating support (though one that cannot be constantly kept in view) of all theory. Although we must already understand that we cannot expect *the* truth from science, we would like at least to know why we wanted to know what we now find ourselves disappointed in knowing. In this sense, metaphors are fossils that indicate an archaic stratum of the trial of theoretical curiosity—a stratum that is not rendered anachronistic just because there is no way back to the fullness of its stimulations and expectations of truth.

The riddle of metaphor cannot be understood solely in relation to difficulties in the formation of the concept. What is enigmatic is precisely why metaphors are "tolerated" at all. The fact that they appear in rhetoric as "ornaments of speech" may be attributed to their choiceness, but that they are also accepted in objective contexts seems to require explanation. In such a context, metaphor is first of all a disturbance. If we follow phenomenology in considering consciousness, insofar as it is "affected" by texts, as a structure in which intentionality is accomplished, every metaphor endangers the latter's "normal harmony."

Into the functional transition from merely supposing something to having it fulfilled in intuition,[3] metaphor interposes a heterogeneous element that points toward a different context from the actual one. Now, discursive (that is, not only punctual) consciousness is perhaps in any case a way of "repairing" a disturbance, overcoming a dysfunction of the (organically so trustworthy) stimulus-reaction system. In this connection, it could have been the synthetic processing of stimulus manifolds into "objects"—complexes determinable not only by signs but also by properties—that first made possible behavior that is appropriate to the facts. To repair its disharmonies, to again and again find its way back to the harmony of the data as data of *one* experience, remains the constitutive accomplishment of consciousness, which assures it that it is following reality and not illusions.

To adopt Husserl's terminology, metaphor is, first of all, "resistance to harmony."[4] This would be fatal for the consciousness whose existence depends on its concern for identity; it must be the constantly successful organ of self-restitution. From this we get, even and precisely in relation to metaphor, the rule formulated by Husserl: "Anomaly, as an interruption of the originally harmonious unity of appearance, is included within a higher normality." It is only under the pressure of the need to repair an imperiled consistency that the element that is at first destructive *becomes* a metaphor. It is integrated into intentionality by means of a trick of reunderstanding. Explaining the exotic foreign body as "just a metaphor" is an act of self-assertion: the disturbance is described as an aid. This corresponds, in experience, to the need to incorporate, as part of the total causal system, even the most surprising event, bordering on a supposed "miracle."

To use Quintilian's much-belabored example, it is a disaster for the smooth flow of information when an intention that is initially fixed on a meadow makes the leap—in a manner that surprises because it goes beyond the range of typical expectations—to the predicate: this meadow laughs, *pratum ridet*. The text seems to be done for, as far as its accomplishing something is concerned, until the "excuse" presents itself that no sequence of the expected objective predicates could ever convey the information concerning a meadow that is contained in the one expression that says it laughs. It is beyond the resources of any descriptive language. But it would also be wrong to say that this is already poetry *in nuce*, however many poets have may have made meadows laugh.

Metaphor captures what is not present in the qualities of a meadow when viewed objectively but is also not the subjective and phantastic addition made by an observer who, only for himself, could find the contours of a human face in the surface of the meadow (the game played by observers of the strange natural formations in limestone caves). It accomplishes this by assigning the meadow to the inventory of a human life-world in which not only words and signs but also things themselves have "meanings," the anthropogenetic prototype of which may be the human face with its incomparable situational meaning. The metaphor for this meaning content of metaphor was provided by Montaigne: "the world's face" (*le visage du monde*).

It took one of the most laborious reconstructions of theoretical language just to find the way back again to what is designated by the term "landscape." Metaphor lays claim to an originality in which are rooted not only the private and leisurely areas of our experience—the worlds of strollers and poets—but also the theoretical attitude's laboratory preparations, made foreign to us by technical terminology. In the latter, Quintilian's meadow no longer has anything to laugh about. But it remains the case that not only has what laughing means for us been "carried over," in the past, to a meadow, but this meaning of "laugh" was also enriched and "fulfilled" by the fact that it could reappear in the life-world. The life-world must always already have contained relationships in which intuition was carried over in the opposite direction, so that metaphor's forcing of consciousness could be endured.

Hence, Wittgenstein's 1929 assertion is also valid: "A good comparison refreshes the understanding." Refreshment itself is here a metaphor, standing in opposition to an equally metaphorical exhaustion: the comparison shows more than is already contained within what it is selected for. This is the model of what is claimed for hermeneutics, but in this case it runs in the opposite direction: interpretation does not enrich the text beyond what the author consciously put into it; rather, the alien relationship flows unpredictably into the production of texts. Metaphor's imprecision, now scorned in the rigorous self-sharpening of theoretical language, corresponds in a different way to the maximal abstraction of such concepts as "Being", "History", "World", which have not ceased to impress us. However, metaphor retains the wealth of its heritage, which abstraction must deny.

The more we move away from the short distance of fulfillable intentionality and orient ourselves toward total horizons that can no longer be traversed and fenced off in our experience, the more impressive the use of metaphors becomes; to that extent, the "absolute metaphor" is a limit. "The forest stands black and remains silent"—that is another case of the "laughing meadow," only we are already linguistically more familiar with the forest one does not see for the trees as soon as one enters it. Here, then, there is a "leap" of our intuition. In this respect, the world is a forest we become aware of only as standers within it—"in that dense forest" (*in hac silva plena*), Marsilio Ficino says—and which we cannot see for the trees. The absolute metaphors that have been found for the world no more resolve into qualities and determinable characteristics than this ultimate forest resolves into trees. Nevertheless, it is the forest in which, according to Descartes's simile, we are lost and must decide to follow a "provisional ethics" (*morale par provision*), *because* we have no overall view of it (although, according to Descartes's theoretical program, we can possess one).

The world might be all that is the case and thereby justify its old definition as a "series of things" (*series rerum*); a Cartesian, with his demand for clearness and distinctness, could hardly be satisfied with that. However uncontradictable it may be, though, that would be, of everything that can be asserted about the world, just about the least interesting thing to the cosmologists or the theologians, or even to those who have had enough of interpreting the world and want to move on to changing it. That the world is a book in which one could read or, after laborious deciphering, might finally be able to read is a metaphorical expectation concerning the nature of experience. It is difficult to think it away, out of the life-worldly attitude that precedes and underlies all theory in our history, and it should be kept in mind, looking back, if only because it invites us to see the mere use value of the world, mediated by the instrument of science, as a secondary direction taken by the theoretical attitude. The enthusiasm with which facts are embraced that again give us something to "decipher" in nature, or even seem to introduce the relationship between text and reader into the natural process itself, is atavistic.[5]

The "book of nature" is not merely a subject for topos researchers to collect citations on. It is also an orientation for inquiring back from the actual status of the theoretical attitude toward the world to the giving of meaning, in the life-world, that underlies it. It would be pure romanticism to do this with the intention of reestablishing the position of the reader of the book of nature. The goal is to suspend the taken-for-granted character of the present, which will always seem to contemporaries to be the last word that was to be said on the subject. Also to suspend expectations of meaning whose specificity can now be grasped only metaphorically and whose unfulfillability, when it is not believed in, automatically produces disappointments.

One senses that there is something implicit in every metaphorics that makes it a preferred element of rhetoric as a way of reaching agreement in cases of unattained or unattainable univocity. The process of cognition entails losses. To define time as what one measures with a clock seems sound and is a highly pragmatic way of avoiding disputes. But is this what we have earned since we began to ask what time is?

The assertion that time is not a discursive concept serves the apotropaic gesture that allows Kant to make time, by way of Newton's absolute time, into the a priori form of inner sense. But when Kant introduces temporal determination into his argument in the "Refutation of Idealism" in the second edition of the *Critique of Pure Reason*, it becomes clear that for him, too, the metaphorics of space is fundamental to the intuition of time and cannot be eliminated from it. This may have to do with facts concerning the brain, in which the accomplishments of spatial representation are genetically older than those of temporal representation.

In that case, is the idea of the *fluxus temporis*, the stream of time, also still a necessary metaphorics? Is the sharing of the absolute metaphor of the stream—between consciousness, on the one hand, and the constitution of time, on the other—the connecting thread on whose strength phenomenology declares time to be the original structure of consciousness? Does applying the principle of the conservation of substance to this figuration allow the further step, taken by Otto Liebmann, that consists in "imagining" the ego as "the serene shore, or rather the solidly anchored island, which the stream of events, the *fluxus temporis*, washes over"?

Finally, recall that historically the metaphor of the stream of time was used destructively by Francis Bacon in attacking the assurance that truth was to be the daughter of time; out of this stream, only what was light enough not to sink into the river reached our present position, according to Bacon—the metaphorical proof of tradition's failure with respect to the burden of truth.

Over the entrance to Camille Flammarion's observatory in Juvisy is written: *Ad veritatem per scientiam* [Toward truth through science]. Today, one would hardly put that over the entrance to a university or scientific institution. Why not? Evidently, the phrase assumes that the truth to be attained is not identical with the science through which it is to be attained. That is a differentiation with respect to which our expectations must be termed extraordinarily vague and imprecise and, in spite of all the clarifications in the scientific world, almost confused. In other words, we no longer know exactly why we undertook the whole mighty enterprise of science at all—independently of all its contributions to the viability of our world, which make it indispensable to that viability. This truth is evidently something that, in the language of science itself, through which it is supposed to be attainable, can no longer be expressed and certainly never has been expressed, either.

Seen in relation to the thematics of the life-world, metaphor, including its rhetorically precisely defined short form, is something late and derived. Therefore, if metaphorology does not want to limit itself to the contribution that metaphor makes to concept formation but takes it instead as the guiding thread for consideration of the life-world, it will not get by without inserting itself into the wider horizon of a theory of nonconceptuality. After all, the fact that one can speak of a "laughing meadow" is poetically suggestive only because its aesthetic evidence relies on everyone's having seen it, without being able to say it. The homelessness of metaphor in a world determined by disciplined experience can be seen in the uneasiness encountered by everything that does not meet the standard of a language that tends toward objective univocity. Unless it fits into the opposing tendency, as "aesthetic." This attribute provides the ultimate, and therefore completely unhampering, license for multiple meaning.

Under the rubric of nonconceptuality, we must at least reckon with the fact that the class of the ineffable, too, is not empty. Wittgenstein's *Tractatus*, which begins with the sentence "The world is all that is the case," ends on a prohibition with regard to what is not the case, or cannot unambiguously be said to be the case: "What we cannot speak about we must pass over in silence."[6] This, however, is a prohibition against confusing one thing with another: the inexpressible with the expressible. Everything that is the case has an unambiguous degree of linguistic availability, whose range, however, is not at all coterminous with what can be experienced. Otherwise, we would not read, immediately preceding the concluding prohibition, "There are, indeed, things that cannot be put into words. They *make themselves manifest*. They are what is mystical" (sect. 6.522). This is the establishment, in passing, of a relic that, not falling under the definition of reality, is as it were homeless. It shares this exotic character with the "sense of the world" that must lie outside the world, and even with the characterization of the mystical, which is localized—in contrast to *how* the world is—in the fact *that it is*.

The contrary position has been formulated by Paul Valéry—one of the few modern poets of whom one can say without exaggeration that they were also important thinkers—in his *Mon Faust*: "Whatever is not ineffable has no importance" (*Ce qui n'est pas ineffable n'a aucune importance*). Actually, Wittgenstein also subscribes to the view that even if all possible questions regarding what is the case could be answered, "the problems of life [would] remain completely untouched" (sect. 6.52). In that case, there could be no relationship of grounding between the life-world and the world of theoretical facts. The situation that obtains after all scientific questions have been answered is essentially the one formulated in this proposition: "Of course there are then no questions left, and this itself is the answer" (sect. 6.52). The philosopher, Wittgenstein says later in the *Philosophical Investigations*, treats a question the way he would treat an illness.

The limits of expressibility and inexpressibility are even more widely separated than those of definitional determinacy and imaginative sketching out. What is up for descriptive discussion is not the existence of correlatives of an asserted speechlessness but that of the striving, which is part of the history of our consciousness, to represent inexpressibility itself in language. I have described this on the model of the "explosive metaphorics"[7] that appears in the tradition of the mystical "negative path" (*via negationis*), that is, in the self-representation of the basic embarrassment of every theology, which has to speak about God constantly without having the right to permit itself to say anything about him. Nicholas of Cusa made this a speculative means of representation for his "coincidence of opposites" (*coincidentia oppositorium*). Thus, he invented the explosive metaphor of the circle whose radius becomes infinite, whereby its periphery gets an infinitely small curvature, so that a curved line and a straight one coincide. An intentionality of intuition is overstretched in order to express its futility in itself and, while reaching out, at the same time to retract its overreaching.

It may be surprising that we can still find modern instances of this striking medieval way of putting things. In one of his diary entries, Georg Simmel clarified a particular aspect of modern historical consciousness when he transformed Nietzsche's conception of the eternal return of the same into an explosive metaphor: "The world process looks to me like the turning of an enormous wheel—in the way, to be sure, that is presupposed by the eternal return. Not, however, with the same result—that at some point the same thing really repeats itself; for the wheel has an infinitely large radius; only when an infinitely long time has elapsed (that is, never) can the same thing happen at the same place—and yet it is a wheel, it turns, and in accord with its idea it aims at the exhaustion of the qualitative manifold, without ever exhausting it in reality." We no longer get any sense of the "sad necessity" of using metaphors, of which the Enlightenment philosopher could speak. Even a desperate act of striving to express what has hitherto been unsaid and held to be unsayable—a proposition concerning not a state of affairs but the totality of all states of affairs—can be an incomparable gain, which the author perhaps glimpsed under the command to remain silent, although paradoxes concerning the ambiguity of "life" are not foreign to him, even in his published texts. There is a borderline zone of language, in which putting things down in writing would involve shame, before the public, but the claim to have perceived something is not retracted. Naturally, a philosophy that uncovered the theme of "life" had to repeat once again Heraclitus's early experiences with language.

In this context, the limiting case of the mystical is only a reminder of the fact that nonconceptuality is not congruent with intuitiveness [*Anschaulichkeit*]. It is not correct to say that myth was the homeland of intuition before the odyssey of abstraction. The mythical proposition that everything is surrounded by Oceanus and stems from him is finally no more intuitive than the one that claims that everything developed out of water. Both have their difficulties, as instructions to be carried out by our imaginative powers. Nevertheless, this "translation" carried out by Thales of Miletus is so momentous because in it a proposition appears that is meant to be taken as the answer to a question. This is largely foreign to myth, even if the Enlightenment was fond of regarding myth as an aggregate of naive answers to the very same questions that science had, in the meantime, taken up with incomparable success.

In order to avoid the snares of myth theories here at least, I will try to examine more closely one of the most momentous statements with mythical quality ever formulated, that of the Apocalypse of John: "The Devil's time is short."[8] Knowing how powerfully this statement still affected religiously awakened émigrés, even close to the present day, as Ernst Benz has described, one will initially want to attribute this to the intuitiveness of mythical propositions. But this assumption does not stand up under examination. The apocalyptic/visionary author may have had an image of the way the devil looked; the reader must get this elsewhere, for instance from his experience with paintings that originate more than a thousand years later. What it could have meant to the author's contemporaries, however, that this devil did not have much time, wholly escapes intuition: time, what time? Clock time, calendar time, historical time? Short or long in relationship to what? It is astounding how little material for filling up the imaginative vacuum has been provided by exegesis on this statement. All the same, it is hardly bound to the cultural determinations of its ancestry; it could be translated, with another name inserted, into any language whatever. At the same time, however, one sees that this statement had to change the way people felt about the world. It alarms us indirectly, since it does not repeat the old song that humans have little time but says this of another being who can be counted on to do his best to make use of the time he has left and to deprive all others of it. It is a one-sentence myth, which does not even set our imagination going but is a formula for something that could not have been expressed conceptually: the power that is bent on causing harm to humans is itself operating under the pressure of time. What comes next was announced by the evangelist Luke, in another one-sentence myth, as the vision of the moment when that power's time has run out: "I saw Satan fall like lightning from heaven."[9]

In the service of the history of concepts, metaphorology has categorized and described the difficulties that appear in the field leading up to concept formation, around the hard core of clear and distinct determination, and even in places definitively remote from it. But a historical phenomenology must also attend to decayed forms, which appear after speech that is taken literally, as embarrassment in the face of the demands of realism. In its rejection of all forms of Docetism, theological Christology discovered stringencies of realism that, up to that point, had been unknown, or were at least not capable of being formulated in rigorous terms, when dealing with myths and their allegorical illustrations, with epiphanies and metamorphoses of undetermined degrees of seriousness. The realism of the Incarnation turned indignantly away from the Gnostic suggestion that, in his historical appearance, God merely passed through human nature as water passes through a tube. The background of informal dealing with mythologemes compelled dogma to establish a rigoristic definitiveness in regard to the saving union of God and man. But the exegetical arts of multiplying scriptural meaning already softened this realism, and metaphor is the linguistic form of evading realism's strict demands.

Anyone who prefers not to consider the crisis symptoms of the late Middle Ages in the increasing metaphorization of theological dogmatics can study this avoidance of difficulties in the repetition of metaphorization in our own century, after the phase of excessive demands made by dialectical theology. Demythicization is in large measure nothing more than remetaphorization: the punctual *kerygma* radiates out over a circle of linguistic forms that no longer need to be taken literally. Dogmatic realism had "understood" what Resurrection was supposed to mean; as an absolute metaphor for the certainty of salvation, that is something of which one might well say it is better for it to remain ununderstood.

This sort of reduction to indeterminacy is certainly one of the characteristic properties of sacred texts, which endure by warding off banal literalism, because people credit them with something without examining what exactly it might be. Reducing church languages back to the everyday idiom exposes each text defenselessly to questions. Leaving Latin aside, I ask what would happen to Paul Gerhardt's chorales if one were to translate them from German into German. It is art, not their sacred content, that protects them against such a translation.

So metaphor can also be a late form. In the history of science, nineteenth-century molecularism's loss of reality is a striking example of this. Ever since Laplace, molecularism had expected that the microstructure of matter would turn out to replicate the macrostructure of the universe and would thus be a field to which Newtonian dynamics could be applied. Molecularism developed at a time when there was no prospect of an empirical solution to the problems of the microstructure of matter; it is the expression of the economical assumption that the solar system represents the simplest structural principle of all physical systems. In the other direction, for clarifying the construction of large cosmic systems, such as the Milky Way, this hypothesis had already proven to be a successful projection that could be cashed out empirically—a "Copernican comparative." For this reason, taking the same approach to the smaller world of the ultimately invisible seemed to be following out a single world principle. Analogy is the realism of metaphor.

The destruction of this realism of molecular solar systems was the work, first, of positivism and its reduction of all physical questions to questions of pure analysis, on the model of Euler's and Lagrange's rational mechanics; and then, absurdly, of Maxwell's generosity in interpreting Faraday's "lines of force," where he allowed the understanding to employ any kind of physical comparison. This was the conclusion he drew from realizing that the positivists' insistence that a scientific statement should contain nothing but differential equations and that reality itself was a mathematical structure had come no nearer to reality than the molecularists' Newtonian systems. It was not a question, he thought, of antithetical theories but of the changing occupations of the position of "scientific metaphor." According to Maxwell, human thinking could operate only through intermediaries in the sphere of pure positivity, and in any case could not be satisfied without introducing a metaphor for the symbolics of calculus.

This procedure was doubtless governed by the principle of insufficient reason. Thus, Wittgenstein was once again to describe philosophy as based on preferring certain comparisons without having sufficient reasons for selecting them. In general, many more conflicts among people are due, he says, to the "preference for certain comparisons" than at first appears.

The objection that metaphorology, and still more a theory of nonconceptuality, has to do with irrational decisions and that it leads us in the direction of Buridan's ass is a natural one. Even if this were true, it would not produce this state of affairs but would only describe it. But when the theory goes back to the genesis of that state of affairs and analyzes that genesis in terms of a situation of need, something is produced that I would like to call the rationalization of lack. It consists in supplementing the consideration of what we should do to fulfill the intentionality of consciousness, with a—more anthropological—consideration of what we can afford in the way of fulfillments.

In a fragment first published in 1959 by H. Sembdner, Kleist proposes to divide human beings into two classes: "those who are at home with metaphors, and those who are at home with formulas." There are too few people who are at home with both, he says, to make up a class. This typology looks as though it contains an exclusive choice. But in fact we cannot avoid metaphors where formulas are possible. We can afford the abundance of metaphors that our rhetoric produces only because what formulas are able to accomplish determines the scope we have for what goes beyond the bare securing of existence, and thus also the scope for what metaphors offer us in going beyond the formulaic. Above all, formulas guarantee the connection between the beginning states of processes and arbitrary end states, without presupposing that the intermediate field, or the totality, is empirically objective. Nonconceptuality wants more than the "form" of processes or states; it wants their "gestalt." It would, however, be careless to see in this the proposal of a distinction between intuitiveness and abstraction, which in any case are not identical with metaphor or formula, symbol or concept. Here there are complex and often contradictory relations to intuition, in particular.

What binds concept and symbol together is their indifference to the presence of what they represent. Whereas the concept tends potentially toward intuition and remains dependent on it, the symbol, in the opposite direction, disengages itself from what it stands for. It may be that the capacity for symbolism arose from the inability to depict, as Freud suggested; or from magic, with its technical need, by dealing with an arbitrary fragment of a reality, to make the latter itself wholly available for its use; or from the disposition toward conditioned reflexes, in which a circumstance that accompanies the real stimulus takes over and retains the stimulus function itself. What is decisive is that this elementary organ of the relation to the world makes possible a turning away from perception and visualization, a free control over what is not present. The symbol's operability is what distinguishes it from representation [*Vorstellung*] and from depiction [*Abbildung*]: not only does the flag stand for the state, which has selected its sequence of colors, but also, in contrast to the state, it can be exploited or desecrated, displayed at half-mast to signify mourning or at a sports event to signify victory, misused for certain ends and held high for others.

It was only at a late date that this capacity for linking together heterogeneous elements allowed us to understand what happens in human cognition and to understand that it is not governed by the natural but ultimately contradictory evidentness of the saying, "like by like." It may have been philosophy's first absolute metaphor when Heraclitus described thinking as fire, not only because fire, for him, was the divine element but because it has the property of constantly taking up what is foreign and transforming it into itself. Atomism misunderstood this as implying that the shape of the fire atom was a ball that contained all other atomic shapes within itself, and hence most precisely represented the soul's properties of moving and knowing. The concept of the symbol—anticipated by the concept of the symptom, in ancient medicine—first made it possible to grasp what happens in perception and knowledge. The secondary sensory qualities do not depict something that is not there, as such, in the thing, any more than the external symptoms depict the internal diseases; both accomplish what they accomplish only because of the constancy of their connection with what they point to.

Through connection with a rare material, money sought to make value present, but it could be connected with the representation of this value only in some reliable manner, for example, through governmental guarantees of its acceptance. But the symbol is powerless to communicate anything concerning its referential object. Hence, it stands for the nondepictable, without helping us to reach it. It maintains distance in order to constitute between object and subject a sphere of nonobjective correlates of thought, the sphere of what can be represented symbolically. It is the possibility of a mere idea having an effect—an idea as the sum of possibilities—just as it is the possibility of value.

Or the possibility of "being." Do we really understand what was meant by Heidegger's fundamental ontological question about the "meaning of being"? We proceed here, as in all other questions about "meaning," by making use of a substitution. For instance, when we ask about the meaning of history, we do not notice how we substitute something else for what we are inquiring about, when we attribute a goal to the course of history and localize this goal in an end state of the historical process that justifies everything that precedes it. In the question about the meaning of being, this is not possible, because what is inquired about is evidently not subject to any alteration, at least so long as there is not yet a "history of being." The trick that helps us, then, is the claim that the question does not need to be answered at all by looking to its object. Rather, we are supposed to possess this answer already; indeed, we consist in nothing other than the possession of this answer. This would be carrying Platonic anamnesis to a higher level, with the difference that this possession manifests itself not in concepts but in the structure of consciousness itself and in the conduct grounded in it. The reformulation of the question about being avoids Platonic anamnesis's path through the concept, by making the understanding of being the essence of Dasein, without having to say what logical "form" it takes. Here, nonconceptuality consists in our thoroughly learning what kind of thing the understanding of being is *not*.

The answer to the question about being can thus be seen as the root form of our modes of behavior, as the summing up of their implications and of what they are implied by. That is why the being of Dasein is care, care implies time, and time implies being. Such an answer relates to none of the objects that we know, nor to their totality as a world like the one in which we live. That existence is being-in-the-world means precisely that the world of this "being-in" is not composed of "objects" but cannot be grasped in metaphors, either.

Only a little supplementary theory is required to help us understand why this possession was able to remain hidden from us for so long, and with such fateful consequences. It is the supplemental theorem of the inauthenticity [*Uneigentlichkeit*][10] of our existence; in Heidegger, it was only later on transformed into a component of his conception of a history of being, which sought to grasp what was earlier called inauthenticity as an episode of the concealment of being, or rather of being's self-concealment. As a historical doom, it had worse consequences than Dasein's failure to be authentic. It turned scientific reason's blindness with regard to the way its possibility derives from a world relationship into a fated state of affairs.

Heidegger posited an enmity between his question about being and positive scientificity, and this enmity was supposed to be more deeply fundamental than that between intuition and concept, between metaphor and formula. But for this relationship, too—and this cannot be overlooked by the evaluation tendencies in this field—it is true that the question concerning the "meaning of being" can affect or even occupy us only because the question concerning the conditions of existence is neither decided nor even influenced by it.

Initially, the trick of assuming that the answer to the question of being has always already been given had presupposed an indissoluble connection between Dasein and that into which it inquires in this way. This connection results in a coupling of Dasein and being that is so constitutively unobjective, and has such a lifelong and "lifedeep" persistence, that Dasein was able to become the very type of the symbol for being, or rather the type of the grounding of all symbols. What I have called "implication," as the schema of the methodological connection between the analysis of Dasein and ontology, is at the same time a prohibition of metaphorics, and also of absolute metaphor. Nothing can be "represented" metaphorically if all elementary modes of behavior toward the world find their original totality in care, whose ontological meaning lies in temporality, which in its turn is probably the unfolded horizon of an ultimate radicality whose designation may be arbitrarily exchangeable. To this, the strictest prohibition on metaphors applied; the language of the "history of being" proves that it could not be maintained.

An interdiction on metaphor also applies to what is designated by the expression "freedom." Because it could be deduced only "as a necessary presupposition of reason," Kant says, freedom is an Idea. Not only is there no experience of the reality of freedom, there is also no possible way of presenting something intuitive corresponding to its Idea. For it alone, Kant expressly denies the possibility of symbolization—in the sense of the concept of "symbol" that he uses in a way that is close to that of absolute metaphorics—"because no example can ever be given of it in accord with any analogy whatsoever." However, the danger of using an absolute metaphorics for the idea of freedom can be discerned in Kant himself, and its grave, necessarily misleading consequences can be seen in the introduction of the concept of transcendental action. This makes it natural to regard as freedom anything that can be represented as a transcendental action of the understanding.

Kant represented the synthesis of transcendental apperception as an operation of the understanding, and the categories of the understanding as the ultimate rules of that operation. In view of the concept of action in the theory of practical reason, can this already or still be called "action"? The theory of practical reason can and must presuppose the identity of the subject, which is the condition of all possible responsibility and imputability; the theory of theoretical reason cannot do this—it shows the identity of the subject precisely *in statu nascendi* [being born]. The understanding is not the subject that makes use of a mode of operation in its actions; rather, it is nothing other than the sum of this regulated operation itself. If one takes literally the linguistic distinction between the understanding and such "actions," then the whole critique of reason—and not merely the critique of practical reason, which as such is naturally also theoretical—becomes practical. If everything, then, is practical and nothing is any longer theoretical, everyone is, indeed, appeased, but nothing has been learned.

No contribution to the understanding of freedom as the foundational condition of morality has been achieved when we learn that the synthesis of representations, itself, is "already" an action of the understanding. However, this misunderstanding is an older one than its recent inventors believe; it already plays a role in Simmel's much-admired interpretation of Kant and subsequently in his attempt, in his philosophy of history, to derive arguments against deterministic historicism from it. Human beings, then, would "make" their history freely, or more freely, because the synthesis of their representations is an "action" of their understanding. This is just the misleading effect of an absolute metaphor that has been taken literally.

Notes

Translator's Introduction

1. On "self-assertion," see Hans Blumenberg, *The Legitimacy of the Modern Age*, trans. Robert M. Wallace (Cambridge: MIT Press, 1983), pt. 2.

2. "Paradigmen zu einer Metaphorologie," *Archiv fur Begriffsgeschichte* 6 (Bonn: Bouvier, 1960).

3. Translator's introduction to *Work on Myth*, trans. Robert M. Wallace (Cambridge: MIT Press, 1985), p. ix.

Shipwreck with Spectator

1. Aristippus the Cyrenaic most fully, and perhaps first, exploited the illustration of states of mind by the degree of movement of the sea; typically, he was also one of the transmitters of the travel anecdote about the "shipwreck of the philosophers" (frag. 301, ed. Mannebach). The Pyrrhonians and Epicureans had similarly made "calm on the high seas" (*galenótes*) into a metaphor of merely negatively (because of the exclusion of ominous factors, such as wind and storms) determined well-being: *Happy is he who lives*

undisturbed there and (. . .) finds himself in peace and becalmed on the sea. (Sextus Empiricus, *Adv. Math.*, 11:141; further references in H. Hossenfelder's introduction to *Sextus Empiricus, Grundriss der pyrrhonischen Skepsis* [Frankfurt, 1968], 31.) On the metaphor of calm on the seas in Epicurus and the history of its effects, see also W. Schmid, "Epikur," in *Reallexikon für Antike und Christentum* 5 (1961): cols. 722, 805–806. [Unless otherwise indicated, all notes are the author's, with the exception of a few references, which I have supplied. Trans.]

2. Thales was quoted verbatim by Seneca, although he left no writings: "The disc is supported by this water, he says, just as some big heavy ship is supported by the water which it presses down upon" (*hac, inquit, unda sustinetur orbis velut aliquod grande navigium et grave his aquis, quas premit. Naturales quaestiones*, trans. Thomas H. Corcoran [Cambridge: Harvard University Press, 1972], 6:6). Nietzsche already pointed out the noteworthiness of this quotation (Lectures on "*Die vorplatonischen Philosophen*" [1872], in *Gesammelte Werke*, Musarion edition, 4:273). See also Seneca: "[Thales says that] this round of lands is sustained by water and is carried along like a boat, and on the occasions when the earth is said to quake it is fluctuating because of the movement of the water" (. . . *ait enim terrarum orbem aqua sustineri et vehi more navigii mobilitateque eius fluctuare tunc cum dicitur tremere. Naturales quaestiones*, 3:14). The criticism of this is disarming: "That this analogy is not relevant was already clear if one realized that earthquakes are regional events." (G. Patzig, "Die frühgriechische Philosophie und die moderne Naturwissenschaft," *Neue deutsche Hefte* [1960]:310)

3. Hesiod, *Erga*, in *Sämtliche Gedichte,* trans. W. Marg (Zurich, 1970), 618–694.

4. [Here, as elsewhere in this book, the German word translated as "distance" (*Distanz*) implies psychological or aesthetic detachment and not simply spatial separation. Trans.]

5. Erasmus gave some examples of this under the rubric *Isthum perfodere* (*Adagia,* 4:4:26): the futility of the effort confirms nature's resistance.

6. Including leading hecklers into chains of associations. An example from the German Bundestag (reported by R. Zundel, *Die Zeit,* 4 April 1975): in the budget debate, a delegate who belonged to the ruling coalition described the steady course taken by the ship of state, thanks to the coalition forces, and compared the opposition with worried passengers who need to take a catch-up class on navigation, so that they might one day return to the captain's bridge. The opposition shouted back: "We are not in one boat!" Speaker: "I'm talking about the ship of our country, and you are on it, too!" Interruption by Wehner: "He is a blind passenger!" Opposition heckler: "You'll soon go aground if you continue in this way." After the speaker returned to the same metaphor in concluding his address: "For this ship is on the right course, and so that it may sail safely on . . . ," he heard a final cry as he was leaving the podium: "And you are the ship's gremlin!" A classic example of the way metaphors direct, lead, and mislead, or in any case push further and guide a chain of associations.

7. Concerning the ship-of-state allegory, which I will not pursue further here, see Eckart Schäfer, "Das Staatschiff. Zur Präzision eines Topos," in *Toposforschung,* ed. P. Jehn (Frankfurt, 1972), 259–292. For a jurist's view, see H. Quaritsch, "Das Schiff als Gleichnis," in *Recht über See. Festschrift für Rolf Stödter* (Hamburg, 1979), 251–286.

8. Horace, *Odes* 1:3, 23.

9. "Brashly challenging every law, / Mankind plunges ahead into forbidden things." (*Odes*, 1:3, 25–26; *The Complete Works of Horace*, trans. Charles E. Passage [New York: Ungar, 1983], p. 132.

10. Diogenes Laertius, 7:1:2.

11. Vitruvius, *De Architectura,* 6:1–2, ed. V. Rose, p. 130: *namque ea vera praesidia sunt vitae quibus neque fortunae tempestas iniqua neque publicarum rerum mutatio neque belli vastatio potest nocere.* Attention to the status of the shipwrecked person who has been rescued is part of the tradition of Homeric allegorical interpretation: Odysseus on the Phaiakian beach, disfigured by the salt water, frightening away the maids; Athena has to intervene with Nausikaa, taking the fear from her limbs. It is only because the Phaiakians live on the edge of the world and have never experienced enmity toward strangers (because they know no strangers, living as far away as they do!) that they are friendly to Odysseus.

The allegorical interpretation offered by Basil the Great, Bishop of Cappadocia in the fourth century, sees this differently; it is virtue that overlies nakedness: "Homer calls on us in the same way: You must be concerned with virtue, which even swims out with the shipwrecked man, and lends him an appearance that commands respect, even if he comes onto the shore naked." (*Ad adolescentes* 4; *Patr. Gr.* 31, 572)

Pascal will later interpret the situation as a comedy of mistaken identity: a man shipwrecked on the shore of an unknown island is taken by the inhabitants for their lost king, because of his accidental resemblance to the latter; he sees his opportunity and allows all honors and privileges to be showered on him. How does this man see things? He cannot forget his "natural condition," and although he recognizes the necessity of continuing to play his role as king, he is simultaneously aware of the contingency of his success. One line of thought determines his outer state, the other his inner state: "It was through the former that he dealt with the people, and through the latter that he dealt with himself." (*Trois discours sur la condition des Grands*, 1) On this see Hans Blumenberg, "Das Recht des Scheins in den menschlichen Ordnungen bei Pascal," *Philosophisches Jahrbuch* 57 (1947): 413–430.

12. E. R. Curtius has already shown for Latin poetry that the perspective in which the totality of life represents itself affects the poet's self-experience in a special way: "The Roman poets are wont to compare the composition of a work to a nautical voyage." (*European Literature and the Latin Middle Ages*, trans. Willard R. Trask [New York: Bollingen, 1953], chap. 7, sec. 2) There follows a "brief selection" of instances of this. Richly revealing here is what is *not* mentioned: in all the risks run by sailors because of inexperience, the fragility of their boats, cliffs, churning seas and storms, there seems to be no aesthetic shipwreck. That sort of thing is for philosophers.

13. Kästner, *Gesammelte poetische und prosäische schönwissenschaftliche Werke* (Berlin, 1841), 3:82. Not only Kästner's human being but already his God is not merely "distinguished" (in comparison to the Christian God) by mathematics; he is even freed of boredom: "The narrow range of delights at the Court, where, if Voltaire is to be believed, boredom often yawns between Majesties, disappears when confronted by the changes offered to a man who understands mathematics. To depict these changes is to depict everything that is contained in the sensible world—the work of a

---

Creator whom Plato declared to be an eternal geometer, and thereby undoubtedly formed a conception of him more worthy than the Christian philosophers who make this Creator act without any ground."

14. [*The Complete Essays of Montaigne*, trans. Donald M. Frame (Stanford, 1958), 1:38, 177. Subsequent references cite this edition. Trans.]

15. *Complete Essays of Montaigne*, 2:9, 763.

16. *Complete Essays of Montaigne*, 3:9, 764.

17. *Complete Essays of Montaigne*, 2:17, 489.

18. *Complete Essays of Montaigne*, 2:13, 458.

19. *Complete Essays of Montaigne*, 2:13, 458.

20. *Complete Essays of Montaigne*, 2:13, 458.

21. *Complete Essays of Montaigne*, 2:14, 473: "The ancient mariner spoke thus to Neptune in a great tempest: 'O God, you may save me if you will; you may destroy me if you will; but I shall still hold my rudder straight.'" (Paraphrasing Seneca, Ep. 85.)

22. *Complete Essays of Montaigne*, 3:1, 601.

23. *Complete Essays of Montaigne*, 3:1, 601. [Translation modified. Trans.]

24. *Complete Essays of Montaigne*, 3:12, 801.

25. *Complete Essays of Montaigne*, 3:1, 599. [The quotation from Lucretius is on the next page. Trans.]

26. Goethe, *Werke*, ed. E. Beutler, 23:875. But this Goethe who handles the shipwreck metaphorics with such a light touch here, was for modern existential thought always too far removed from all seriousness of peril. Thus Ortega y

Gasset, in an often-cited lecture given on the occasion of the hundredth anniversary of Goethe's death, "In Search of Goethe from Within," expressed the demand, even the condition of an acknowledgment of relevance, in this way: "Give us a Goethe who is shipwrecked in his own existence, who is lost in it and never knows from one minute to the next what will become of him." (In José Ortega y Gasset, *The Dehumanization of Art and Other Writings on Art and Culture,* trans. Willard R. Trask [New York: Doubleday/Anchor, n.d.], 134)

27. *Werke,* 23:663–664.

28. Nietzsche, *The Gay Science,* trans. Walter Kaufmann (New York: Vintage, 1974), 3:124, 180–181. Regarding the "existential" finality of the embarcation metaphor, see also Goethe's earlier formulation: "I am now wholly embarked upon the waves of the world—fully resolved to discover, achieve, struggle, shatter, or to explode into the air with all my freight." (Letter to Lavater, 6 March 1776) That is what already in the *Urfaust* links the night monologue, in view of the earth spirit's sign, as the feeling of courage to risk oneself in the world, with the metaphor of shipwreck: "With storms to strike about me/ And in the shipwreck's grinding not to be afraid." (An exclamation mark was first inserted in the version of *Faust* as "A Tragedy.") "Storm and Stress" is indeed nothing but one of early forms of the "existential." But the prior metaphorical imprinting of the embarcation image then also makes it possible to relate to it along with its corruption. Without his relationship to Nietzsche, Georg Simmel would not have been able to announce in such terms, on 9 December 1912, his turn toward his friend Marianne Weber's "life philosophy": he was now shifting his sail, he said, and seeking untrodden

land, but without much hope, since the voyage would "probably not end on the coast." In any case, what happened to so many of his companions (in time and profession) was not to happen to him: "they made themselves so much at home on the ship that they ended up thinking the ship itself was the new land." (Max Weber, *Lebenserinnerungen* [Bremen, 1948], 385)

29. *Werke*, 14:144–145.

30. Karl Josef Lamoral de Ligne, *Neue Briefe*, trans. V. Klarwill (Vienna, 1924), 46.

31. *Werke*, 6:101.

32. *Werke*, 6:90.

33. Franz Overbeck, *Christentum und Kultur. Aus dem Nachlass*, ed. C.A. Bernouilli (Basel, 1919), 136.

34. *The Gay Science*, 1:46, p. 110.

35. *The Gay Science*, 4:289, p. 232.

36. *Werke*, 20:148.

37. *The Gay Science*, 1:45.

38. *Anthologia Graeca,* 9:69, ed. H. Beckby (Munich, 1965–1967), 3:38–39.

39. Casanova, *Geschichte meines Lebens*, trans. H. v. Sauter, 4:104. The distich is used here in the fifteenth-century version by Ianus Pannonius: *Inveni portum. Spes et fortuna valete: / Nil mihi vobiscum est: ludite nunc alios* (*Geschichte meines Lebens*, 113). The adventurer replies to the abbot that this is the translation of two Greek lines by Euripides, "but perhaps they apply here once again, Monsignor, for I have altered my view since yesterday."

40. Alain René Lesage, *Histoire de Gil Blas de Santillane* (1724), vol. 9, chap. 10.

41. Lucretius, *De Rerum natura*, 2:550–568.

42. *De Rerum natura*, 5:222–227.

43. *De Rerum natura*, 5:999–1006.

44. *De Rerum natura*, 5:1430–1435.

45. *De Rerum natura*, 5:1226–1240.

46. "Little soul, like a cloud, like feather, / My body's small guest and companion, / Where now do you rest, in what places— / Stripped naked, and rigid, and pallid, / Do you play as before, little jester?" (Trans. Elinor Wylie)

47. *Entretiens sur la pluralité des mondes*, 3d discourse.

48. Voltaire, *Zadig*, chap. 20. "Everything in this world is dangerous, and everything is necessary."

49. Mme du Châtelet, *Discours sur le bonheur*, ed. R. Mauzi, 3.

50. Voltaire, *L'A B C ou Dialogues entre A B C. Quatrième Entretien sur la Loi Naturelle et de la Curiosité. Oeuvres complètes* (Basel, 1792), 50:278–284.

51. "Pardon, Lucrèce, je soupçonne que vous vous trompez ici en morale comme vous vous trompez toujours en physique. C'est à mon avis, la curiosité seule qui fait courir sur le rivage pour voir un vaisseau que la tempête va submerger. Cela m'est arrivé." (*Oeuvres complètes*, 56:62)

52. J. Orieux, *Leben Voltaires* (Frankfurt, 1968), 2:106. [Voltaire had offended the Prussian king, Frederick the Great, by his attacks on Maupertuis, and left Berlin in March

1753. From May until July, he was detained in Frankfurt by Freytag but finally escaped to the Palatinate. Trans.]

53. "On the basis of my own experience and that of all my fellow gawkers, I think people rush to every kind of spectacle only out of curiosity."

54. *Voltaire's Correspondence*, ed. Theodor Bestermann, no. 16303d: "J'avoue que le morceau `curiosité' de Voltaire est superbe, sublime, neuf et vrai. J'avoue qu'il a raison en tout, si ce n'est qu'il a oublié de sentir que la curiosité est une passion, ou si vous voulez une sensation qui ne s'excite en nous que lorsque nous nous sentons dans une parfaite sécurité de tout risque. Le moindre péril nous ôte toute curiosité." I have discussed Galiani's letter from another point of view in *Die Legitimität der Neuzeit* (Frankfurt, 1966):409; *The Legitimacy of the Modern Age* (Cambridge, Mass.: MIT Press, 1983):406.

55. F. Schalk, ed., *Die französischen Moralisten*, 2:60.

56. The reference to Ewald's "Der Sturm" is from Otto Seel, "Zur Ode 1.14 des Horaz. Zweifel an einer communis opinio," in *Festschrift Karl Vretska* (Heidelberg, 1970): 204–249. The poem is reprinted in *Deutsche Epigramme*, ed. G. Neumann (Stuttgart, 1969).

57. On the obligatory commentators' question as to whether the poet imagines his "I" to be on the ship or on the shore, O. Seel, "Zur Ode 1.14 des Horaz": 229, has made the essential points: "Concerning the question as to whether 'Horace' 'was' on board the ship or on land, every position is wide of the mark. Instead, the question is simply this: whether the 'I' who becomes active with a special responsibility in the superior function of 'warner' participates in the

suffering and perils of the event, or whether by fate it represents valid truth and wisdom, as the voice of valid reason and insight as opposed to the interested blindness and involvement of the actors, whose eyes are prevented from recognizing their true situation. Neither beach nor shore have anything to do with it."

58. Quintilian, 8, 6:44. *Allegoria . . . totus ille Horati locus, quo navem pro re publica, fluctus et tempestates pro bellis civilibus, portum pro pace atque concordia dicit* (The whole passage in Horace is an allegory, in which the ship stands for the state, waves and storms for civil wars, and the port for peace and tranquility). In opposition to the penetrating effect on later authors of "Quintilian's rather embarrassingly mechanical solutions," O. Seel has referred to the contradiction that the poet cannot simultaneously speak "from outside" and mean the "ship of state." Rather, he argues, "the more we allow his image-language to operate on its own terms, the higher the rank" the poem holds ("Zur Ode 1.14 des Horaz": 214, 241). Of course, one should then be careful in using the expression "allegory," which always suggests unambiguous coordinate relationships. If one begins by asking, "How, then, is the allegory in Ode 1.14 to be interpreted?" this seems to block the methodological path that would allow one to answer: "I would think: not at all" (*op. cit.* 245).

59. A. Kiessling, quoted in Seel, "Zur Ode 1.14 des Horaz": 221. The Alcaeus fragment (fr. 86 A) goes something like this: "I can no longer determine the direction of the wind: For the wave rushes toward me now from this side, now from that; and in the midst we sail on in the dark ship, fighting hard against the storm's violence; for the waves are already flowing over the base of the mast, and from the tattered sail huge pieces are blown forlornly away."

60. O. Seel, "Zur Ode 1.14 des Horaz": 237–238.: "In the case of Alcaeus, one speaks quite spontaneously in the preterit, whereas in Horace's case, one speaks just as involuntarily in the present tense: Alcaeus reports retrospectively a past event; in Horace we have a present, mimetically represented event." The observation continues: "The poem does not come to an end, it merely stops; the concern takes the form of a general principle, and while the admonitory, threatening voice does not address a concrete ship, and certainly not a crew, it does address the lyric *you* that is always so important for Horace."

61. *Journal meiner Reise im Jahr 1769* (Erlangen, 1846); quoted from *Sämtliche Werke*, ed. B. Suphan, 4:1878.

62. *Auch eine Philosophie der Geschichte zur Bildung der Menscheit*, ed. H. G. Gadamer (Frankfurt, 1967):48. Gadamer calls this "earliest historicist manifesto" also a "bitter satire against the Enlightenment's pride in reason" (146–148).

63. *Briefe zur Beförderung der Humanität*, in *Sämtliche Werke*, ed. B. Suphan, 18:314ff.

64. *Rückblicken über mein Leben* (1847).

65. Knebel's translation of the opening of Book 2 of *De Rerum natura* must be quoted here for the content of the scene: "It is sweet to witness from the distant shore the distress of others in the raging winds on the high-surging seas; not that one can delight in other people's misfortune but rather as long as we see from what difficulties we are free."

66. [Goethe was not present on the battlefield. The question refers to his experience when Napoleon's troops occupied Weimar after their victory. Trans.]

67. *Werke*, 22:454.

68. Nietzsche, *Beyond Good and Evil*, trans. W. Kaufmann (New York: Random House, 1966), p. 178 (sec. 244).

69. "Moralische Erzählungen und Idyllen von Diderot und S. Gessner," *Werke*, 14:157.

70. H. Bräuning-Oktavio, *Herausgeber und Mitarbeiter der Frankfurter Gelehrten Anzeigen* (Tübingen, 1966), 407.

71. I am grateful to Fritz Schalk for the information that editions of Voltaire's letters were available to Goethe even before the appearance of the Kehl edition in 1773 and that he could have "supplemented" the motif of the spectator in bed.

72. ["gerade zum Schutze *seiner* Geschichte vor *der* Geschichte." Trans.]

73. ["Vulcanism" (or "Volcanism") and "Neptunism" refer here to competing geological theories concerning the process of rock formation. Neptunism had its roots in antiquity and held that all rocks were formed in the sea. Trans.]

74. Hegel, *Die Vernunft in der Geschichte*, ed. J. Hoffmeister (Hamburg, 1955), 78–81. [I have followed, for the most part, H. B. Nisbet's translation of this work: *Lectures on the Philosophy of World History. Introduction: Reason in History* (Cambridge: Cambridge University Press, 1955). Trans.]

75. Letter from Goethe to Chancellor Müller, 20 February 1821, *Werke*, 22:122.

76. Erasmus, *Adagia*, 2,3,2: *De his, qui denuo sollicitantur ad subeundum periculum.* M. Hecker ("Ein unbekanntes Goethisches Gedicht," *Goethe-Jahrbuch*, N. F. 3 [1938]: 227–232) suggests as Goethe's source for this saying Andreas

Schott's *Adagia et Proverbia* (Amsterdam, 1612). This work is mentioned in Goethe's diary for 21 May 1797, considerably too late for the poem written in 1781, since other evidence of Goethe's use of Schott's collection is lacking. On the other hand, Hecker overlooks the evidence of familiarity with Erasmus found in Goethe's recommendation to Schiller, on 16 December 1797, to "get a copy of Erasmus's *Adagia*, which is easy to find." The *Adagia* was in Goethe's library (*Goethes Bibliothek. Katalog*, ed. H. Ruppert [Weimar, 1958]:209). Just how inaccessible the allusion to the "figs" of the adage was, in fact, is shown by the bewilderment with which the first publisher of the poem, Philipp zu Eulenburg-Hertefeld, in 1897, read, against the clearly written holograph, "Zurück ins Meer, das wieder steigen will" ("Back into the sea, which wants to rise again"). Hecker's further assumption that the discovery of the adage in Schott first reminded Goethe of the still-unpublished poem from 1781 and moved him to revise it as "Abschied" ("Farewell"), must at least also be applicable to Erasmus's *Adagia*. In "Abschied," the hungry sea is no longer in the background but only the softly *rocking boat of sweet foolishness*, as the vehicle of separation.

77. Letter to Duke Karl August, Naples, 27–29 May 1787 (*Werke*, 19:78). On the voyage out to Messina, Goethe had made the decision to complete his "Tasso," and to oppose the formal constraint of verse to the "weakness and fogginess" of the prose version begun in 1780. What was thus decided on the sea of the Sirens' rock ended in the great metaphor of the rock and the waves, by means of which Tasso compares himself with Antonio, as a sinking man implores the rescuer: "So klammert sich der Schiffer endlich noch / Am Felsen fest, an dem er scheitern sollte" ("So the

sailor finally clings still / To the rock, on which he was to shipwreck").

78. Goethe, *Aus meinem Leben. Dichtung und Wahrheit*, 3, chap. 15; *Poetry and Truth*, trans. John Oxenhandler (London and Chicago, 1974), 2:298. [Translation slightly modified. Trans.]

79. Schopenhauer, *Die Welt als Wille und Vorstellung* (1816), 1, sec. 16; *Sämtliche Werke*, ed. W. V. Löhneysen, 1:38. [This and all other passages quoted from this work are here given in the English translation by R. B. Haldane and J. Kemp. Trans.]

80. *Die Welt als Wille und Vorstellung*, 3, sec. 39.

81. *Die Welt als Wille und Vorstellung*, 4, sec. 58.

82. Schopenhauer, *Nachlass*, ed. A Hübscher (Dresden, 1816), 1:427–429. —The misanthrope as worldly-wise sailor: *Nachlass* (1814), 1:199.

83. *Nachlass* (Dresden, 1818), 1:489; cf. *Die Welt als Wille und Vorstellung*, 4, sec. 57 (*Werke*, 1:429), where another passage from Book 2 of Lucretius's poem is quoted.

84. [The German word *Schauspiel* (drama, theater) contains within it the notion of looking (*schauen*), just as the word "theater" is derived from the Greek root *thea* (viewing), which is also the etymological source of "theory." Trans.]

85. *Die Welt als Wille und Vorstellung*, 1, sec. 16 (*Werke*, 1:139).

86. *Die Welt als Wille und Vorstellung*, 4, sec. 63 (*Werke*, 1:482). Nietzsche will cite this passage at the beginning of the *Birth of Tragedy*, in order to describe "the wise quiet of the sculptor-god," of which, "in an eccentric sense," what

Schopenhauer says of "man caught in the veil of maya" is true: Apollo is "the magnificent divine image of the *principium individuationis*," distant from the horror and intoxication of Dionysus.

87. [A report or a memorial. Trans.]

88. *Ludwig Börne. Eine Denkschrift. Sämtliche Schriften*, ed. K. Briegleb, 4:34–35.

89. Jerry Allen, *The Sea Years of Joseph Conrad*, German trans. (Wuppertal, 1969), 218.

90. *Weltgeschichtliche Betrachtungen* 6, *Werke* (Darmstadt, 1956), 4:195–196.

91. *Historische Fragmente*, ed. E. Dürr (Stuttgart, 1942), 194–211. I also refer to parts of the draft that were cut out by Burckhardt, 248–254.

92. From the winter semester of 1867–68 also come the listeners' notes on the lecture "Über die Geschichte der Revolutionszeitalters," on the basis of which Ernst Ziegler proposed his "reconstruction of the spoken text" (Basel, 1974).

93. Letter to Andreas Heusler-Ryhiner, 30 July 1844. Jacob Burckhardt, *Briefe*, ed. M. Burckhardt, 2:110.

94. *Weltgeschichtliche Betrachtungen* 4, "Die geschichtlichen Krisen," *Werke*, 4:128.

95. *Historische Fragmente*, 251–253.

96. Emil Du Bois-Reymond, *Darwin versus Galiani* (Berlin, 1876), 23.

97. Emil Du Bois-Reymond, *Über die Grenzen des Natur-erkennens. Die sieben Welträtsel. Zwei Vorträge* (Berlin, 1884),

79. Reprinted in *Vorträge über Philosophie und Gesellschaft*, ed. S. Wollgast (Berlin, 1974), 169–170.

98. [The "jenseitige Lager" not only are on the other side in the debate about evolution but are believers in "the other side"—the supernatural. Trans.]

99. Paul Lorenzen, "Methodisches Denken," *Ratio* 7 (1965):1–13. Also in Lorenzen, *Methodisches Denken* (Frankfurt, 1968), 24–59.

100. O. Neurath, "Protokollsätze," *Erkenntnis* 3 (1932/ 1933):204–214.

Prospect for a Theory of Nonconceptuality

1. Hans Blumenberg, "Paradigmen zu einer Metaphorologie," *Archiv für Begriffsgeschichte*, 6 (1960):7–142.

2. [On "absolute metaphor," see Blumenberg's "Paradigmen zu einer Metaphorologie," p. 9. Trans.]

3. ["*zu anschaulicher Erfüllung.*" Here and elsewhere I have translated *anschaulich*, *Anschauung*, and related words by "intuitive," "intuition," etc., in accord with the use of such terms in Husserlian phenomenology. Trans.]

4. [*Widerstimmigkeit*]

5. [On the "book of nature," see the author's *Die Lesbarkeit der Welt* (Frankfurt am Main: Suhrkamp, 1981. Trans.]

6. Ludwig Wittgenstein, *Tractatus Logico-Philosophicus*, trans. D. F. Pears and B. F. McGuinness (London: Routledge and Kegan Paul, 1961), sects. 1, 7. Subsequent references appear in the text.

7. [*Sprengmetaphorik*. Cf. Blumenberg's "Paradigmen zu einer Metaphorologie," pp. 132: "What we would call

'explosive metaphorics' . . . draws concretization into a *process*, in which it is at first able to follow along (e.g., conceiving a circle's radius doubled and ever further increased), but finally reaches a point (e.g., conceiving the greatest possible, that is, infinite, radius of a circle) where it has to give up—and this is understood as 'giving itself up' as well." Trans.]

8. [Revelation 12:12: "But woe to you, O earth and sea, for the devil has come down to you in great wrath, because he knows that his time is short!" Trans.]

9. Luke 10:18.

10. [It is perhaps worth noting here that *Uneigentlichkeit* also means "figurativeness," and *Eigentlichkeit* (opposed to it in the following sentence) also means "literalness." Trans.]

Index

Vulpius, Christiane, 50

Studies in Contemporary German Social Thought
Thomas McCarthy, General Editor

Jürgen Habermas, *The New Conservatism: Cultural Criticism and the Historians' Debate*

Jürgen Habermas, *The Philosophical Discourse of Modernity: Twelve Lectures*

Jürgen Habermas, *Philosophical-Political Profiles*

Jürgen Habermas, *Postmetaphysical Thinking: Philosophical Essays*

Jürgen Habermas, *The Structural Transformation of the Public Sphere: An Inquiry into a Category of Bourgeois Society*

Jürgen Habermas, editor, *Observations on "The Spiritual Situation of the Age"*

Axel Honneth, *The Critique of Power: Reflective Stages in a Critical Social Theory*

Axel Honneth, *The Struggle for Recognition: The Moral Grammar of Social Conflicts*

Axel Honneth and Hans Joas, editors, *Communicative Action: Essays on Jürgen Habermas's* The Theory of Communicative Action

Axel Honneth, Thomas McCarthy, Claus Offe, and Albrecht Wellmer, editors, *Cultural-Political Interventions in the Unfinished Project of Enlightenment*

Axel Honneth, Thomas McCarthy, Claus Offe, and Albrecht Wellmer, editors, *Philosophical Interventions in the Unfinished Project of Enlightenment*

Max Horkheimer, *Between Philosophy and Social Science: Selected Early Writings*

Hans Joas, *G. H. Mead: A Contemporary Re-examination of His Thought*

Michael Kelly, editor, *Critique and Power: Recasting the Foucault/Habermas Debate*

Hans Herbert Kögler, *The Power of Dialogue: Critical Hermeneutics after Gadamer and Foucault*

Reinhart Koselleck, *Critique and Crisis: Enlightenment and the Pathogenesis of Modern Society*

Reinhart Koselleck, *Futures Past: On the Semantics of Historical Time*

Harry Liebersohn, *Fate and Utopia in German Sociology, 1887–1923*

Herbert Marcuse, *Hegel's Ontology and the Theory of Historicity*

Larry May and Jerome Kohn, editors, *Hannah Arendt: Twenty Years Later*

Pierre Missac, *Walter Benjamin's Passages*

Gil G. Noam and Thomas E. Wren, editors, *The Moral Self*

Guy Oakes, *Weber and Rickert: Concept Formation in the Cultural Sciences*

Claus Offe, *Contradictions of the Welfare State*

Claus Offe, *Disorganized Capitalism: Contemporary Transformations of Work and Politics*

Claus Offe, *Modernity and the State: East, West*

Claus Offe, *Varieties of Transition: The East European and East German Experience*

CPSIA information can be obtained at www.ICGtesting.com
Printed in the USA
BVOW06s0442191115

427555BV00002B/7/P